ILLUSTRATIONS FOR PREACHING

BENJAMIN P. BROWNE

ILLUSTRATIONS
FOR
PREACHING

BROADMAN PRESS
Nashville, Tennessee

4222-28
ISBN: 0-8054-2228-5

Dewey Decimal Classification: 808.88
Subject heading: ILLUSTRATIONS

Library of Congress Catalog Card Number: 76-39713
Printed in the United States of America

PREFACE

A confirmed believer in the use of stories to illustrate the winsome power of the gospel—a method of the Master—I offer here many new and a few cherished illustrations suited to sermons for today.

Through serving in pastorates and in a ministry reaching across our country, I employed a wealth of apt illustrations which I am happy to share. Inevitably I am indebted to a host of preachers and public speakers as well as to my own experiences and wide reading for the illuminations presented here.

I hope those whose stories I pass on will be as generous in sharing as I have been in giving my illustrations. Since it is impossible to thank personally all who in some way over the years have contributed indirectly to this compilation, I here offer them my sincere thanks. The illustrations that have been shared with me have been distilled through my own mind; therefore, their expression has taken on something of the coloring of my own thinking. In some cases, perhaps in many, I like to think they are expressed more dramatically and effectively.

Specifically, I acknowledge the courtesy of Fleming H. Revell Company in granting me permission to quote from my book, *Let There Be Light.* I also owe thanks to *The Secret Place, Baptist Leader,* and *Time of Singing* for permissions to quote. To the Judson Press, I acknowledge permission to quote from *52 Story Sermons.*

I have adapted two or three illustrations from my book *Gateway to Morning.* Other permissions may appear infrequently in the book.

For his literary labors in correlating and organizing the materials of this book I owe special thanks to Rev. Charles A. Waugaman, poet and pastor of South Haprsmell, Maine. For helpful criticism and encouragement my thanks are due to Dr. William J. Craven of La Jolla, California, to Dr. Donald Reiter of Santa Ana, California, and to Rev. D. M. Morrison of Los Angeles. For the work of typing my manuscript I thank Marilyn Dodson, Betty M. Kopye, and Lois Pebley. This book is sent on its mission with fervent prayer that it may help many pastors to illuminate the glorious gospel of our God and Savior, Jesus Christ.

BENJAMIN P. BROWNE

CONTENTS

1.
Sources

Where You Can Get Illustrations

"Where do you get your illustrations?" asked an acute young pastor, himself in search of sermon pictures. "Everywhere!" The answer may not seem very helpful, but it is the truth. A certain clairvoyance of soul can keep the heart, the eyes, the ears searching like so many bees among the flowers. Wide reading will bring home to the mental hive the distilled fragrance of far fields.

One should keep watch on his own mind in its adventures as well as in its leisure moments. One should listen much, learn humbly, and not always be talking. In the Temple Jesus was *listening*.

Think As You Walk

On his walks in Northampton, Jonathan Edwards would snatch a piece of paper from his pocket, scribble down what had just popped into his mind, and then pin the paper to the outside of his overcoat. By the time he returned to the manse after a three-mile walk, his coat, sprinkled with white papers, looked as if he had been through a snowstorm of very large flakes. John Hutton said his best ideas always came to him while he was walking. For the same reason, Phillips Brooks carried a pocket notebook in which he wrote ideas, phrases, and vivid impressions.

Whether you carry a notebook or not, you do carry with you in the memory of your experiences the best book of sermonic illustrations that has ever been written. This chapter should point out these overlooked sources of effective illustrations. If you will give your own experiences the flair of imagination, the force of graphic portrayal, and a creative application to spiritual insights, you will be following biblical precedents. In his earthly ministry Jesus used common scenes and everyday experiences to illuminate the most profound religious truths, and so did Paul. If you discover hidden spiritual truths in sports, gardening, travel, events of the times, automobiles, friends, and other objects and experiences, you will be following a divine pattern.

For example, make use of your travel.—Paul, traveling in Athens, used a special statue he had seen as the subject of his Mars Hill sermon. If you can say, "I was driving a car up a road in Galilee toward Nazareth" you will have arrested the attention of your audience. But if you have never been to the Holy Land, it *can* be just as effective to say, "We were in a party climbing snowcapped Mount Hood in Oregon" or "I was driving on Main Street through a little western town when a cowboy . . ." "Walking on Fifth Avenue in New York I passed . . ." "In the crooked streets of Boston, looking for Paul Revere's house, I got lost . . ." "In West Virginia I saw the appalling scars of strip-mining . . ." The possibilities of travel are endless. You see beauty, tragedy, poverty, youth, lakes, mountains, slums, animals. Use them just as Jesus used a fig tree, a mountain, and a meadow of bright flowers. They invite comparisons with spiritual illustrations.

Make use of your auto and your experience with cars on the road.—The auto is probably the most common link in modern life binding us all into a single interest. The frustrating dirt on the windshield proves to be dirt on the inside. Is the new model car half as important as a new man in the car? The flat tire tests your patience; the traffic jam raises your blood pressure; and the big truck ahead of you on the curves of the two-lane mountain road tells whether your anger turns to rage or profanity. The sudden failure of brakes can be a moral symbol. Then there are skidding, time payments on the car, accidents, obsolescence, dead spark plugs (maintain your spiritual glow, said Paul), an empty tank five miles from the nearest gas station, neglect to get a tune-up, dirt in the carburetor—with all these situations the congregation will quickly identify incidents that have happened to them. It takes only a spark of imagination to convert these events into parables of religious living.

Make use of sports also.—You have in your congregation recreation enthusiasts who love football, golf, baseball, tennis, hockey, basketball, bowling, car racing, and whatnot. These sports are replete with illustrations. Paul watched the games and contests in Greece and often urged the early Christians to strive like athletes. He saw the training, the goals, the striving for mastery, the discipline, the rewards, the disqualified, the victors, and the vanquished. In our modern world there is an array of athletic illustrations from which to choose. Then there are the champions and heroes, the Christy Mathersons, the Babe Ruths, the Hank Aarons, the Lombardis, the Palmers, and the Billie Jean Kings.

Make use of your childhood and youth.—Jesus made points by illustrations about children's games, both when the children played "weddings" and mourned at "funerals." Events of your childhood vividly recall nostalgic memories in your congregation. Remember the thrill, unless your family was affluent, of your first pair of skates, the new shoes, the new suit, and the first money you earned? The excitements of Thanksgiving, Halloween, and Christmas can never be forgotten. Remember when you decided to run away from home? The resentment of that hard punishment? Your first bicycle, your fifth-grade teacher, and the girl in the sixth grade you fell madly in love with? Then there were the relatives—uncles, aunts, cousins, and grandparents—all with oddities. How about the day your baseball broke a neighbor's window and your dog was accused of tearing up a neighbor's garden? Go on to high school and the sports program, graduation, and choosing a college. What a vast volume of illustrations uniquely your own are at hand, awaiting the magic of your touch to appear as exciting highlights to Kingdom truths.

Make use of your friends.—This is one area that might be overlooked unless it is mentioned here. You will not, of course, violate confidentiality, disclose information given in counseling sessions, or embarrass your friends. But your powers of invention should be given freedom to tell a story of a friend while successfully concealing his identity. The friend is in a remote parish of some years ago. You also have a host of casual friends whom you met on the train, the plane, the ship, at a convention, or at a sports event. Something unique, special, odd, eventful, striking relates to one of these friends. You can generally describe him safely and anonymously without fear of libel, saying, "I have a friend" or "I met a friend at a football game."

To press the matter even further, though some will disagree, you have the same literary license as the novelist or the teacher who uses a character in a parable. Here is a preacher who wants to illustrate the modern news mania. "I have a friend," he says, "who had six different daily newspapers delivered to his door, and twelve varieties of newsmagazines. Then he listened to television news at breakfast, at lunch, and at dinner. He had disaster for breakfast, catastrophe for lunch, and calamity for dinner. Finally he got so uptight and so depressed that he unplugged his television, stopped all newspapers and magazines, and refused to hear any news outside his home." This friend was doubtless fictional or partly so, but the illustration it developed was effective and illustrated a modern dilemma. The imagination has untapped resources.

Capture the Vivid Impressions

You will be "hit between the eyes" by a sudden scene, idea, impression, personality, bit of news, experience, or human situation. Capture that transient moment of vividness by writing it down while it is still burning inside your mind.

Look for the Dramatic in the Bible

In your reading of the Bible, you will discover many dramatic actions that will lie all around your feet, like the sparkling colored stones on the seashore, so avidly gathered by eager-eyed children. That verse or story which knifed into your own heart and conscience during your private reading can be a stirring voice of conviction in your pulpit or classroom on Sunday. If it made you smart, use it. "I preached what I did feel, what I did smartingly feel," said John Bunyan, who could gather four thousand people to hear him at five o'clock in the morning in London.

Look for Dramatic Contrasts

You are reading the Psalms. "He telleth the number of the stars; he calleth them all by their names" (147:4). Your mind leaps with a solar sweep to the dizzying thought of illimitable space and to the immeasurable greatness of God. Earlier in the psalm you read with amazement, "He healeth the broken in heart" (147:3). The psalmist in the same breath passes to God's illimitable power from his careful concern for the individual soul. He is at once the almighty Creator who upholds shining worlds and the merciful Father who bends in love over broken hearts.

Search for Surprises

You are reading Psalm 119, where the psalmist listed 165 wonderful qualities about the divine Lord. Along with enumerating these marvels of divine wonder that elicit his praise, the psalmist revealed his humble desire when he prayed, "*Open* thou mine eyes, that I may behold wondrous things out of thy law" (v. 18). The psalmist felt that he stood only on the threshold of divine truth, that as yet he knew almost nothing of the wonder of God. He hoped and prayed for new discoveries and fresh unveilings of God. Are these not the qualities needed by Christians?

Word Pictures of Jesus Always Hold Attention

No drama equals the story of the woman taken in adultery. Here are sin, love, forgiveness, condemnation, conscience, hypocrisy, and hope all pressed into moments of breathless suspense. To analyze sincerely the subtle human qualities of this scene, as well as the compassion of the divine Redeemer, is to discover anew that the Bible is after all the supreme handbook of illustrations for the preacher of the gospel.

Read the Newspaper—But Standing Up

Current reading will build windows on wide horizons if one selects wisely. In the entire nation, there are probably only three or four newspapers worthy of a minister's brief spare time. The foreign correspondents' columns or the editorials may open a new casement from your castle tower. Ministers had better read the newspaper standing up, lest it steal priceless time.

The News of the Week Is Yours to Use

The news of the day was not unimportant to our Lord. How adroitly he used a contemporary disaster to contrast a spiritual truth. "Or those eighteen, upon whom the tower in Siloam fell, and slew them, think ye that they were sinners above all men that dwelt in Jerusalem? I tell you, Nay: but, except ye repent, ye shall all likewise perish" (Luke 13:4-5). If the big news of the week has a spiritual lesson, it can be thundered from the pulpit. We may well take a leaf from the Book of the supreme Teacher. The nearby mountain, the visible stones of the Temple, the redness of the evening sky, the notorious robberies on the Jericho Road, the birds that sang overhead, the fruitless tree, the grapevine at the porch, and the flowers in the field all came as inspired, poetic touches to enliven his eternal pictures.

Don't Overlook the Power of Simple Illustrations

Nor did he miss the stupendous significance of the simple. A woman turning the house upside down in search of a lost coin—well, has no woman in your church ever told you of an experience like that? A father watching for a son to come home—the homes of America have often quivered with the agonized longings of parents for sons coming home from the battlefields. Has such a scene melted your heart, too? Then tell it as best you can, although you may never approach the story of the returning son in Luke 15. Did you ever watch a farmer sow his spring-plowed acres? Thousands of us have, but only Jesus could make it a centuries–retold masterpiece of parable and could inspire painters like Millet, who based his canvas *The Sower* on Jesus' story. Jesus' insight discovered the stupendous in the simple. Don't be afraid to ponder and use simple things. A famous seminary president gave one of his most impressive addresses when he talked to a group of four hundred men on "Christ, the Bread of Life" and took a freshly baked loaf of bread into his pulpit for illustration. At the close of his talk, four men asked to join the church. Ernie Pyle endeared himself to millions by daring to share his understanding of the common, slugging foot soldier. He let others write up the generals.

Cull the Best from the Best Magazines

Aside from religious journals, there are scarcely more than a half-dozen magazines that are worth a busy pastor's time.

For instance, I remember reading an article on "Revolution in the Cornbelt" by Kurt Steel. I picked up the fact that not only is the origin of corn a mystery to the most acute botanist, but that corn is absolutely dependent on man's help for its very survival. Corn is one of man's most essential foods and greatest helpers (it is rich in minerals used in the mass production of penicillin), yet only by man's care and attention can corn survive at all. When an ear of corn falls to the ground, the tight wrapping of husk keeps the single kernels from sprouting. If accidentally they do sprout, they crowd with so many others in the earth that they starve each other out; and if one fights its lone way up, it will be only a straggling runt unable to bear seed for a second generation of corn.

Thus, although corn is a benevolent gift of God to man's need, it is singularly dependent on man's cooperation. Man and God, with the seed, actually do become co-workers in every harvest of corn. By means of this cooperation the American farmer each year plants acres of corn which, if they were all put together, would total the size of California. Here is a vivid picture for either your sermon on "Co-workers with God" or your sermon on "The God of Harvest."

Visit Art Galleries and Museums

Visit art galleries wherever they are available, for the painters, like the seers and the poets, often penetrate into reality.

Read Poems

Read poetry to give you inspiration, imagination, color, sensitivity, and insight. But quote poems sparingly. The American people as a whole are not poetic-minded. Nevertheless, there are pictures for you in Robert Frost, T. S. Eliot, and W. H. Auden among contemporary poets as well as in E. A. Robinson, Tennyson, and Browning, to mention but a few.

"Bring Me the Books"

Books are gold mines for the digger. "Paul has not lost his delight in books even when he is near his death," said John Calvin. He alluded to Paul's counsel, "Give attendance to reading" (1 Tim. 4:13), written from his prison cell in Rome. Down to the moment that he prepared for death, Paul was still the book lover. There is his touching message to Timothy as the aging apostle pleads, "The cloak that I left at Troas with Carpus, when thou comest bring with thee, and the books, but especially the parchments" (2 Tim. 4:13). Paul left no doubt in any mind that Christian preachers and teachers ought to be readers.

Of course, there is always the danger of reading too much and thinking too little. Too much reading, however, is not a fault that many American pastors have time to acquire. "Sell your shirt and buy books" was the advice of Dr. Alexander Whyte of Edinburgh. There is no better counsel for a man who wants to be rich in illustrative material than the admonition of Paul, "Give attendance to reading."

Listen to Great Preachers and Speakers

Never miss a chance to hear a great preacher. Quote him later if you must; but better still, discover what new trails of thought he blazes for you and follow these through to your own mounts of vision. If he penetrates to the depths within you by some lines of poetry or some moving picture, you may afterward candidly ask for the privilege of using his illustrations or poems. He may even offer to send them to you, but never reproduce verbatim unless you are quoting poetry. Let the beauty and force of what you have heard become a part of yourself. In the end, you may make better use of some illustration than the original giver. Whatever you borrow from another, stamp with your own personality and express with your own words.

Make Notes of Your Reading

Every book worth reading will leave you not only with pointed ideals, but also with painted pictures. Make your notes on the margins of the book and arrange those pictures on blank pages at the beginning of the book into a private art gallery which you may quickly review at any time.

In Boston I bought a biography of Milton which I found autographed by Dr. George A. Gordon, the famous pastor of the New Old South Church. He had written all over the pages of this book his impressions, and he had written an outline of a lecture on Milton. I was proud to possess a book that had inspired one of his great lectures and to discover one of his personal methods. There is little gain in owning a book if you cannot mark it up and make it give you its best. Only be sure that your congregation gets the gospel every Sunday and not a digest of the latest book you have been reading. Some congregations always know exactly what their pastors are reading every week by listening to their sermons. It is just as well not to let your reading become a sore thumb to your congregation.

2.
How to Use the Stories

The Best Things in the Worst Times

A minister is moved to inspire his people in times of despair to carry on courageously in the highest hope and the best faith. Suppose he would have them keep a candle burning, even in the darkest depths. The following introductory story will serve him well.

In the church at Leicestershire, England, there is a memorial tablet inscribed to the honor of Sir Robert Shirley. This is what it says: "In the year 1653 when all sacred things throughout the nation were either demolished or profaned, Sir Robert Shirley, Baronet, founded this church, whose singular praise it is to have *done* the best things in the worst times and *hoped* them in the most calamitous." In the destructive times of the English civil war, when hatred and cruelty were rife, Sir Robert Shirley simply determined to do something constructive; so he built a Christian church. Precisely the time to do good is when times are bad. The worst times are exactly the times when God must count on his disciples to do the best things.

The World for Christ

It may be that a minister desires to preach a sermon on the signs of our times, on the Christian world mission, or on the social implications of the gospel. Then he may find the following illustration a helpful introduction.

In order to broaden the mind of his little son, a father purchased a globe of the world. He set it in the boy's bedroom where the boy might twirl it about and thus gain some conception of the shape of the world, its oceans, and its continents. By providing his son with an early acquaintance with the world, the father hoped to broaden and expand the mind of his young son. Indeed, the boy gained a kind of affection for this globe that stood on the table in his room.

After the boy had gone to sleep one night, the father wanted to look up the longitude of Shanghai, China. He crept slowly up the stairs and walked on tiptoe into the boy's room, took the globe into his hands, and was tiptoeing out the door when the creak of his footstep wakened his boy. The boy sat bolt upright in bed, rubbed his eyes, and asked, "Daddy, what are you doing with my world?"

That is a fair question for every father, to every citizen, to every church member: "Daddy, what are you doing with my world?" What kind of a world are we preparing for our children to live in? Earth might be fair. What are we doing with our Father's world and the world of God's children?

Beware the Rocks Near Home

It may be that a minister wants to point up a sermon on personal religion or to emphasize the danger of the shipwreck of character in the daily and familiar round. The following story may serve him:

The coast of Maine has many harbors and many dangerous reefs. Near Portland, just off Cape Elizabeth, there lies a rocky reef that is just inside the harbor. It is called Trumbie's Reef, named after an old sea captain who was brought up as a boy on Cape Elizabeth, joined the crew of a ship at an early age, and put out to sea. He sailed around the world and became the captain of a large ship. His skill as a world sailor became famous. He piloted his ship through many a stormy voyage and into many a dangerous harbor. Rich and famous, he sailed back to his home port in Maine. Here he felt at perfect ease. He was familiar with the outline of the shore and with every rock and reef. Yet as he sailed into the harbor, his ship grounded on this small reef and suffered shipwreck. Afterward the reef was known as Trumbie's Reef. The captain could sail the seven seas safely, but he piled up on rocks inside the harbor close to home. The great issues in life we conquer, but small things and the daily round often bring us disaster.

The Cross Central

A pastor preaching a sermon about the cross, emphasizing its centrality, may wish to direct the attention of his people back to the cross. He could begin his sermon:

In the National Art Gallery in Washington, D.C., the gift of Andrew Mellon to the nation, one views the original of Raphael's *The Alba Madonna*, painted in 1510. The colors of the painting are ravishing. The design is a blending of all figures into the rhythm of a circle. The significant thing about the picture, however, is not the beauty of the landscape, the charm of the Madonna, or the innocence of the Christ child. The significant thing is that all eyes are fixed upon the cross upheld in the hands of the child Jesus.

Is this an artist's fancy or profound insight on the part of the flawless Raphael? The eyes of Holy Writ are focused upon the cross. Today we center our vision upon the cross of Christ. "All the light of sacred story gathers round its head sublime."

Friends

Occasionally a man may also wish for an introductory story for some occasion other than that of a sermon. He may have a club or community address. He may desire to give a talk on friends or friendship. He can begin with this:

Josh Billings said, "I'd rather have a million friends than a million dollars, for if I ever did get hard up they ought to be good at least for a dollar apiece." Indeed, friends are priceless; and I am glad to make new friends today.

Or the preacher may be giving an address on the dignity of human life or the significance of man. A single sentence from William James will give him a start.

Dignity of Man

William James was much impressed by the man who washed windows at the Philosophy Hall at Harvard. James was discussing men with him one day when the window washer remarked, "There is not much difference between one man and another, but what there is makes a lot of difference."

Imagination Makes a Difference

Suppose a minister wants to preach on the subject "Imagination Present." He may find this story helpful. A small boy sat solemnly by the side of a pool fishing. "What are you fishing for, little man?" asked a man who was passing by. "Sharks," replied the boy. "But there are no sharks in that pool, my little man," said the stranger. "There ain't any fish in the pool at all," answered the child, "so I might as well fish for sharks as anything else." Everything depends upon one's imagination.

Faith

A man may wish to preach on the peril of unbelief or upon the greatness of faith. Sir Wilfred Grenfell said, "The best definition of faith I know is reason grown courageous." A good introductory sentence is that by Gladstone, who said, "The mark of greatness is not how little but how much a man believes in." Great believers are as rare as great poets, great artists, or great musicians. But the great discoverers were men of faith; the great scientists were men of faith; and the great adventurers have always been men of faith. Another definition of faith is: "Faith is the act of belief in reality, not accessible to sense perception." Dr. Alexander Whyte said, "God is, and is whether we believe or do not believe, but he is for us only real to the extent that we have faith, that we appropriate him." Josiah Royce of Harvard gave this famous definition: "Faith is the soul's discovery of some great reality that enables a man to stand anything that can happen to him in the universe."

Many persons have the wrong idea of faith, not unlike that of the little boy in Sunday School who said, "Faith is believing something that you know ain't so." That people do have difficulty defining faith was noted by Dr. John Broadus, to whom a colored preacher said, "Faith is jess faith. Tain't no more'n faith. Tain't no less'n faith. It's jess faith." Christopher Columbus wrote, "For what the human spirit alone cannot attain God grants to men, for God is wont to enable his servants and those who love his law to perform incredible things." When Daniel Webster knew that death was near he wrote his own epitaph for his tombstone in Marshfield, Massachusetts. It begins, "Lord, I believe. Help thou mine unbelief." (See Mark 9:24.)

Immortality

Immortality may be the theme of a sermon with this introductory story:

When the visitor goes to the famous Christ Church at Fifth and Arch Streets in Philadelphia, he will see the grave of one of America's geniuses and one of the world's greatest men, Benjamin Franklin. The quiet cemetery is walled off from the streets' traffic din, and in a quiet spot one may observe the flat stone over Franklin's grave. Strangely enough, it bears no trace of the epitaph that Franklin composed for his monument:

> Like the cover of an old book,
> Its contents torn out

And stripped of its lettering and gilding,
Lies here food for worms.
But the work shall not be lost
For it will—as he believes—appear once more
In a new and more elegant edition
Revised and corrected by the Author.

3.
Christian Life in Action

The Sand Traps of Life's Game

Golfers rightly fear the hazards of sand traps, yet few can avoid them completely. At some time our course in life will catch us in the adversity of a sand trap. The danger is that we may be unprepared to deal with the tough situations in life.

Arnold Palmer, the famous golf champion, said on one occasion that over the years he had watched hundreds of golfers practicing. He had observed them meticulously practicing putting—the easy, short putts on the soft velvet grass—and he had watched them practice the swing down the thoroughfare, but in all his lifetime and experience, he had never once seen a golfer practicing how to get out of a sand trap.

Jesus said, "In this world ye shall have tribulation, but be of good cheer. I have overcome the world" (John 16:33). For the Christian, there is a way out—"I can do all things through Christ which strengtheneth me" (Phil. 4:13).

Strife—Process

Everyone may win who tries, for the struggle is the prize.

Strength and Weakness

Our True Security Is in God

In an age when many forms of security are promised us by the secular world, it is important not to be taken in by spurious forms of security. In a changing world of chaos, the Christian must look for eternal security to his God and heavenly Father.

One of the stories often told is that of the answers made by a Christian who was standing charges before an angry Roman Emperor. "I will banish you," raged the emperor.

"You cannot," the Christian replied, "for the whole world is my Father's house."

"Then I will slay you," said the emperor.

"Neither can you do that, for my life is hid with Christ in God. I fear not them who have power only to destroy the body but have no power to destroy the soul."

"Then," retorted the emperor, "I will take away your treasure."

The Christian responded, "You cannot do that, for my treasure is in heaven where moth and rust do not corrupt."

Frustrated, the emperor finally said, "I will drive you away from man, and you shall have not a friend left to be near you."

The Christian quietly affirmed, "No, you cannot do that either; for I have a Friend from whom you cannot separate me. There is nothing you can do to harm me for neither life nor death nor things present nor things to come can separate me from his love."

A Favorite Illustration of Arnold J. Toynbee

Hearing the world-famous historian, Arnold J. Toynbee, speak, one discovers that Toynbee loves to tell how one North Sea fisherman had a secret way of landing his catch of herring fresh into the London market.

Often the problem for the typical North Sea herring fishing boats was how to keep the herring fresh and alive until the boat reached the distant port of London. Singularly enough, one of the fishermen invariably had success in landing his catch of herring in London fresh and alive. Finally the other fishermen, who were mystified, asked him how he did it. "Ah, that is a secret," he replied. Under the joshing pressure of his fellow fishermen, however, he finally was led to disclose his secret.

"Well," he said, "into each barrel of herring that I pack I put a catfish." "But," the other fishermen objected, "doesn't your catfish eat the herring?" "Oh, yes," replied the successful fisherman, "the catfish eats just a few herring; but you ought to see how the other herring swim for dear life. They just keep swimming around as lively as tadpoles, and they are as fresh as a rose in June when I get them to London."

Perseverance

Dr. William H. Prescott, noted historian and author of the classic books *The Conquest of Mexico, The Conquest of Peru,* and many others, had to work under great disability. As a Harvard student his left eye was destroyed when a fellow student hit his eye by hurling a hard crust of stale bread. This so injured the other eye that he became all but blind.

He had to write with movable screens at his window to dim the light. His writing was done on a special instrument called a noctograph, a framed device with wires for lines, and he used a stylus to make words on carbon paper. For many years he could write only one hour a day, often only in half-hour periods, sometimes in only ten-minute periods. With painful discipline he trained his memory to retain all that was read to him until his brain had marshalled a tremendous amount of vast historical material. At only a snail's pace he plodded on courageously with unremitting perseverance. "I must make my brain serve for my eyes," he said. When he died at age sixty-three, he left the world sixteen voluminous books of classic historical significance, and he was acclaimed a historian without peer.

He Spared Not His Own Son

The brutal Spanish Civil War tore Spain apart and dragged on for three years, 1936-39. There were bitter loyalties on both sides of the conflict.

Alcazar, the fortress at historic Toledo, loyal to Spain and the church, held out when all the rest of the city had been overrun by the Spanish Republican armies. Colonel Moscado was the stubborn defender of the Alcazar.

General Cabello, of the besieging forces, unable to get Moscado to surrender, telephoned Colonel Moscado that if he did not surrender in ten minutes, he would shoot his son, whom he held captive. To prove that his trust was not a fraud, Cabello said, "I will let you speak to your son Luis."

Luis came to the phone and said only one word, "Papa."

"What is happening, my boy?" his father asked over the line.

"Nothing," was the simple answer of the boy; "they say they will shoot me if you do not surrender the Alcazar."

There was a moment's hesitation. "If it be true," Colonel Moscado replied to his son, "commend your soul to God, shout 'Viva Espana,' and die like a hero. Good-bye, my son; a last kiss."

"Good-bye, Father," answered Luis, "a very big kiss."

"The Alcazar will never surrender," shouted the father. Luis was executed forthwith. The Alcazar held out to a final victory.

Success or Failure

"Our business in the world is not to succeed but to continue to fail in good spirits."—*Robert Louis Stevenson*

Emerson wrote, "My entire success, such as it is, is composed of particular failures."

The Challenge of Handicaps

"I Am Blind Too"

Dr. George Claghorn tells us of a young man, a friend of his, who became blind and was sent for special training to the seeing eye institute for the blind at Morristown, New Jersey.

He was met by another young man and taken to his room. This young man said, "Now I am putting your suitcase down in this corner of the room. Over on this side of the room is the bureau; there is a drawer for your neckties. Here is a drawer for your shirts. Now here on this side of the room is your bed. Over there is the door and stairs where you will come down to dinner. The bell will ring at exactly six o'clock; then you go out of that door, come down these stairs, turn to your right, walk along the corridor, and you will come to the dining room." Then the young man said, "Now I will leave you."

"But," exclaimed the newcomer, "you can't leave me. I am all in the dark. You forget that I am a blind man and cannot see."

The young stranger, who had been holding on to him, said, "I am blind, too."

At that very moment, said Dr. Claghorn, his friend suddenly gained self-confidence. He realized that he was not alone in the world with his experience or darkness and that if others could find their way, surely he could, too.

Albert Einstein's Experience

As a baby, Albert Einstein worried his parents. His head was overly large for his body, and he did not begin to talk until he was three years old.

As a young man he was turned down on his application for a teaching position in physics.

Once Mrs. Einstein, his wife, was visiting the world's largest telescope center at Paloma, California. The director took special pains to explain to her in great detail all the intricate, mathematical procedures of the great telescope and what it revealed of the stars. She listened a bit impatiently and then remarked, "Oh, my husband worked all that out on the back of an old envelope."

The Hardships of the Great

Whitman was half paralyzed, his body clamped to an invalid chair at age fifty-four. Bravely struggling, after three years he learned to walk again, only to be hit at age sixty-five by a sunstroke, followed by another seizure which left his arms and legs "turned into gelatin." Then he had another stroke, followed by two more, until his mind wandered. Yet he spoke of the "grandeur and exquisiteness of old age." On his sixty-ninth birthday he could speak of "undiminished faith" and of "the jocund heart yet beating in my breast." Dragging himself from his chair to his window in his small room, he held on to life until age seventy-three.

Cervantes, author of *Don Quixote*, lost his left hand in the battle of Lepanto. Providentially, his right hand was saved for the writing of his great literary works, but he was imprisoned, suffered great poverty, and barely escaped the auto-da-fé.

Renoir, the French Impressionist, could not walk after age sixty. A paralytic stroke so handicapped him that a servant had to squeeze his paints onto the palette for him. A paintbrush was fastened to his wrist and then fixed on his finger. He was pushed to his canvas in a wheelchair. Yet he painted prodigiously until death claimed him at age seventy-eight.

Make Your Problem into a Profit

Disneyland in California and Disneyworld in Florida provide fantastic entertainment as business enterprises operated for profit.

Disneyland confronted a problem when every visitor went home as soon as it got dark. Here was a big loss of revenue. How could they make people stay over and spend their money at night? Their "think tank" came up with the idea of an electric parade—a spectacular pyrotechnical display. Now everyone who goes to Disneyland advises others, "Whatever you do, don't miss the electric parade." It is held at 10:00 P.M., so people stay, buy dinners, shop, and spend their money for several hours longer. The problem solved became a great money-maker for Disneyland.

Disneyworld in Florida, after the expenditure of millions in building a vast and excitingly new entertainment center, stumbled into a problem also. It was of a different sort from that in California. In Florida a rainy day cut attendance way down, and profits took a big loss.

Once more leaders were called to bat ideas around until a solution was found. The answer to the problem was "the Rain Paradise " For every rainy day, a marvelous, exciting, colorful, fantastic "Rain Parade" drew the crowd, and profits shot upwards. Now everyone says, "Don't stay home when it rains, or you will miss the most wonderful parade you ever saw." The rain problem was turned into a big profit.

We are "more than conquerors" if we only knew it and turned our problems into challenges for benefits.

The Pessimist

The Maine farmer is known to be pessimistic, and with good reason, since his soil is thin and his weather atrocious. On a bright, sunny morning a tourist said to a Yankee farmer, "What a magnificently beautiful day!" The farmer shook his head and said, "It's a weather breeder. Likely brings a bad day tomorrow." The tourist turned his head and saw the farmer's flourishing cornfield, the golden tassels gently tossing in the soft summer's breeze. "My goodness," observed the tourist, "you certainly are going to have a bumper crop of corn." "Yes, maybe," the farmer agreed reluctantly, "but that kind of a crop is pesky hard on the soil."

Retort to Doubters

A doubting Thomas asked the Bishop Sheen, "Bishop, do you really believe that Jonah was in the belly of a whale for three days?" Sheen replied, "I don't know, but when I get to heaven I'll ask him." Doubting Thomas said, "But suppose Jonah won't be in heaven, what then?" Sheen answered, "I'll let you ask him."

Life Consistent with Preaching

One day St. Francis promised his company of disciple monks that they should go out into the village around and preach. He led them from the cloister of the monastery and said, "Brothers, let's go down into the town and preach." Following close behind the venerable Francis they wound their way down the streets of the town, round the lanes, and through the outskirts of the town to the village beyond. Finally they ended back at the monastery where they had started.

Then the boldest of the young monks said, "But you told us we were going out to preach. When shall we begin to preach?"

Francis looked upon them and said, "My brothers, we have been preaching all the time we were walking. We have been preaching in the streets and in the marketplace and in the shop and in the rain. We have been observed; our behavior was marked; and so we delivered a morning sermon for Christ. My sons, it is of no use that we walk anywhere to preach unless we preach as we walk."

4.
Evangelism

Evangelism of Youth

On the occasion when the late D. L. Moody was conducting meetings in England, he returned home one night to his friend's house, where he was staying. His friend said to him, "Well, how many were converted tonight in the meeting?"

"Two and a half," replied Moody.

"Why, what do you mean?" asked his friend. "Was it two adults and a child?"

"No," replied the evangelist, "it was two children and an adult. The children have given their lives to Christ in their youth, while the adult has come with half of his life."

He Still Lives

A Christian missionary was being challenged by a very sincere Mohammedan inquirer. "You know," he insisted, "when we Mohammedans go to Mecca, at least we can find the coffin of Mohammed, our great prophet. But when you Christians visit Palestine, all you find is an empty grave."

The missionary, not at all disturbed by this pointed argument, merely suggested: "That is just the difference. Mohammed is dead and still in his casket. All other religious leaders are dead; but Jesus Christ, whose kingdom includes all nations and all races of different colors, is not in a Palestinian grave. He is risen from the dead and lives and rules forever." It was this faith that filled the early disciples.

Fellowship of the Concerned

Albert Schweitzer told of an operation performed in his hospital on the edge of the primeval forest at Lambarene in Africa. After the operation was finished, Dr. Schweitzer sat in a dimly lighted dormitory and waited for the man to awaken. As soon as the man recovered consciousness, he stared about him and exclaimed: "I've no more pain! I've no more pain!"

Then he took hold of Dr. Schweitzer's hand and would not let go.

The famous missionary began to tell the man and all the others in the room that it was the Lord Jesus who told the doctor and his wife to come to Ogowe. He told them how the white people in Europe gave them the money to make the trip and to work among the sick natives. He explained who the white people are, where they live, and how they know that the natives suffer from disease and sickness. Dr. Schweitzer and the natives sat side by side in the dark room and felt that they truly knew the meaning of the words "And all ye are brethren" (Matt. 23:8).

Let the Master Release the Music

A true story is related about Mendelssohn. He always was eager to play the ancient organs of the great cathedrals of Germany. He had not had opportunity, however, to play the organ of the cathedral at Freiburg.

With the simplicity of great men he wandered incognito into this beautiful cathedral in order to touch the keyboard of the cathedral organ.

Without revealing his identity, he approached the caretaker of the cathedral, announcing that he was a musician and asking if he might have the privilege of playing the organ. It happened that on this particular day there was nothing in his dress or in his approach to suggest his true greatness. With severe abruptness the caretaker, therefore, refused him. When the unknown stranger pressed the caretaker for an opportunity to play just one tune, the caretaker protested that this organ was so priceless that no one but master musicians were allowed to lay a hand upon its console. It was, therefore, unthinkable that this wandering musician should be granted such a right.

With a polite patience, however, Mendelssohn persisted in his request until he had overcome the resistance of the caretaker and won him at least to a reluctant permission. "Very well then, you may play just one small tune on the organ and no more." To enforce his limited permission the caretaker went up and stood beside the stranger as he played.

Mendelssohn began moving his long slender hands upon the keyboard slowly and mildly, feeling out the quality of the notes on the great organ, until he himself was overcome with its richness and let himself go in a burst of glorious symphony. The old caretaker stood aghast and lifted up his eyes to the arches resounding with the cadences of heavenly music; he could hear the whir of angels' wings and the whirling seraphim. The pillars and foundations of the cathedral shook with the thunders of the diapason.

Tears began to trickle down the cheeks of the old caretaker. He laid a hand upon the shoulder of the stranger as Mendelssohn finished playing. He turned his tearstained face to Mendelssohn and pleaded, "Sir, tell me your name."

"My name," modestly answered the master musician, "is Felix Mendelssohn."

Trembling and faint, the caretaker said, "Ah, sir, how can you forgive me? Only to think that I refused you, the greatest musician of Germany, the right to play on this organ. I never dreamed it was such a wonderful organ until I heard you play. Sir, you have brought music out of this instrument that no one has ever dreamed was here before."

So it is with Christ and our souls. There is silent music which has never been released or brought to expression in the souls of every one of us and never will be until we permit Christ to lay his hands upon the keyboard of our lives and we yield to his control. Then will he bring forth eternal music, and possibilities we have never dreamed of will find glorious expression. How tragic to refuse the Master the right to bring forth the riches of melody, the grandeur of immortal music, and the harmony of heaven in your life.

Christ Is Everything

The famous orchestra leader Arturo Toscanini was one time conducting a rendition of Beethoven's Ninth Symphony in London. He directed with so much virtuosity, and all the members responded to his baton in such accord, that at the climactic conclusion of the symphony the London audience's applause sounded like successive rows of thunder.

The first violinist in the orchestra leaned over and whispered to the second violinist, "If Toscanini criticizes us this time for our rendition of this symphony, I'm going to get up and push him backwards into the pit."

He said this because Toscanini was a perfectionist and a disciplinarian as a leader. Instead, to their surprise, Toscanini stood there within the inspiration of the great music—uplifted, exalted, and yet humble. Finally he turned and said to the orchestra, "Toscanini is nobody. I am nothing. You are nobody. The orchestra is nothing," and then he paused. Then, lifting his hands high above his head and pointing toward heaven, he exclaimed, "Beethoven! Beethoven! He is everything!"

And the Christian who has once caught a vision of Christ in his glory and his majesty and then has seen how humble he is by contrast can only exclaim: "I am nobody. I am but a poor sinner. But Christ, he is the Lord of lords; he, Christ, is everything."

Distortion of Values in Our Society

On the night of October 29, 1974 in Zaire, two prizefighters fought eight rounds. In the eighth round Mohammed Ali knocked George Foreman to the mat with such a blow that Foreman could not get to his feet by the count of ten. Both men, the victor and the defeated, collected the sum of $5,000,000 each. The short fight paid the fighters a total of $10,000,000. Mohammed Ali, the champion, announced that at his next fight he would collect as his prize the sum of $10,000,000.

Meanwhile, statistics currently show the average salary of pastors to be $6,500 for twelve months of work. Schoolteachers on the average do only a little better; and, of course, clerks and white-collar workers are generally on very low salaries. Values in our society are upside down and simply ridiculous.

The Power of Love Triumphs

In the Korean War the explosion of a bomb with its blinding flash cost the vision of a four-year-old girl, Kim. The North Korean Communist soldiers invading the land stripped the parents' home and garden of everything. The family of little Kim, with nothing to eat, roamed the streets begging for bread. They could not beg enough food to feed the starving family. In desperation at watching his children starve, the father hurled blind little Kim and her sister into the river to drown. But the mother screamed and howled hysterically until the father was forced into an attempt to rescue the girls. Kim was saved, but her sister drowned.

Christian love had built a missionary orphanage for the blind. Loving friends rescued Kim from hunger and brought her to the orphans' home. Here Kim learned to sing as a child, and she sang songs at Korean revival services.

When Kim was ten years old a Christian couple's love went out to the faraway blind child, and Kim was adopted by Mr. and Mrs. George Wicke of Indianapolis.

In this home she had to learn to master English because her new parents did not know a word of the Korean language. So well did she adjust to life in a new country that she earned her B.A. and M.A. from Indiana University. She won a Fulbright Scholarship and earned a doctorate from the Vienna Institute.

Meanwhile, the diminutive blind Kim had trained her voice to a lovely operatic quality and range. She sang at the Hollywood Bowl on the occasion of Billy Graham's Evangelistic Anniversary and at the World Conference at Lausanne, Switzerland. Those who listen to her lovely soprano voice seldom listen without shedding tears.

It was a long way for a blind, starving child drowning in the river in Korea to come to America and gain the power to move thousands with her deeply spiritual singing—but the love of God carried her all the way. Though she often wondered what the future could hold for her, she said, "It is wonderful to know that God knows the future, and we must be big enough to trust him."

Don't Delay Repentance

The story is told of a famous rabbi who was walking with some of his disciples when one of them asked, "Rabbi, when should a man repent?" The rabbi calmly replied, "You should be sure you repent on the last day of your life." "But," protested several of his disciples, "we can never be sure which day will be the last day of our life." The famous rabbi smiled and said, "The answer to that problem is very simple. Repent now."

The Optimism of the Christian Faith

Jesus read in the humble Simon, the fisherman, the possibility of greatness. He said in effect to him, "You are Simon [a small stone] but you shall become Peter [a rock]." Pascal at his conversion was overwhelmed by "the grandeur of the soul." "What shall a man give in exchange for his soul?" our Lord asked (Matt. 16:26). Jesus never called any man a "worm," yet how often in our false humility we demean the royal status we possess in Christ, who has "made us kings and priests" (Rev. 1:6).

A story was told by Dr. Bob Schuller in one of his television addresses of a pastor of a large church who had a negative self-image. Discouraged, he went into the sanctuary alone, got down on his knees in humility, and prayed, "Oh, God in heaven, I know I am nothing. I'm just nothing."

Just then one of the assistant ministers stepped into the sanctuary and overheard the senior pastor's prayer. So he came alongside and, kneeling, also prayed. "Oh, God in heaven, I am nothing. I'm just nothing."

As this was going on, the janitor entered the sanctuary and, being profoundly moved by the prayers of the two ministers, knelt beside them and joined their prayer, saying, "Oh, God in heaven, I am nothing. I'm just nothing."

The assistant minister looked at the janitor and then, turning to the senior minister, exclaimed, "Now look who thinks he's nothing!"

Christ didn't shed his blood for "worms"; he died because he knew that his love and redeeming grace could produce greatness of soul.

Personal Evangelism

Hand-picked fruit is often the best. Many have been "won by one." John Bunyan, author of *Pilgrim's Progress*, came to Christ by overhearing three women talking intimately with joy of the things of Christ. William Carey, the father of modern missions, was won to Christ by a fellow apprentice shoe cobbler, John Warr. It was an unknown lay preacher who won Charles Spurgeon to Christ in a little chapel on a snowy morning, where only few were present, with the text "Look unto me, and be ye saved, all the ends of the earth" (Isa. 45:22). Afterward Spurgeon said of this preacher, "The preacher was a poor, uneducated man who had never had a training for the ministry and probably will never be heard of in this life. He was a man engaged in a humble business during the week. He was a poor man, a humble shoemaker or something of that sort."

Christ Seeks You

The English poet Francis Thompson emphasized the above truth in his great poem "The Hound of Heaven," in which God is called the Celestial Huntsman. God incarnate in the Lord Jesus is searching for the human soul.

This poem grew out of Francis Thompson's own experience. At eleven years of age he had been sent to college with the expectation that he would prepare for the ministry. His indolence, however, made his father decide that Francis should become a medical doctor. But his years at medical school were disastrous, and he acquired a love for opium and laudanum that brought his life to the brink of ruin. He drifted into London until he became a ragged and unkempt beggar with no shirt beneath his coat and bare feet in broken shoes, living in the slums of that great city. He led a poverty-stricken life, picking up odd jobs occasionally, blacking boots, selling matches, or holding horses. Kindness was shown to him by a poor girl, and he met the poets Master and Mrs. Wilfred Meynell. By their tender understanding and Christian winsomeness, they brought him through Christ into the love of God. Thompson was redeemed and became a writer of Christian poetry.

In "The Hound of Heaven" he pictured his soul fleeing from the pursuit of Christ, the divine lover. At long last Christ caught up with Thompson and held him a spiritual captive.

"You Are My Man"—the Deeper Spiritual Life

No preacher in America moved his generation more deeply than Dr. George W. Truett of Dallas, Texas. His simple eloquence mightily moved great congregations.

Few, indeed, knew the personal tragedy in his life that led him into deeper consecration and became the secret of his power. The story is told in his biography by his son-in-law, Dr. Powhatan W. James. As a younger man Dr. Truett went out hunting on one occasion with some friends. Truett's shotgun discharged accidentally and wounded his closest friend, a chief of police. While the wounded man lingered between life and death, young Truett, together with his whole congregation, interceded for the life of the friend who had been shot. Nevertheless, soon after, Truett saw his friend die.

All that night and for days to come the young pastor wrestled with God in prayer. No light came. He told his wife that never again could he go into the pulpit to preach and that his ministry was ended. He spent long hours with his Bible and repeatedly uttered the words "My times are in thy hands." Late Saturday night he fell asleep. Just before daybreak on Sunday morning there came to him a vision that inspired him to go back into his pulpit to pray and to preach with a fervor and conviction he had never known before.

In his vision he seemed to see Jesus as vividly near as an earthly friend at his side and seemed to hear the Master say to him, "Have no fear. You are my man from now on."

So vivid was the vision that he awakened his wife immediately and told her. He slept again, and the vision was repeated. When he went back to sleep the second time, the vision was repeated for the third time. Something revolutionary happened in the soul of George Truett. "You are my man from now on," said Jesus. Many who heard Truett speak thereafter went away under the conviction of the Holy Spirit, whispering, "Truett is surely God's man."

Give Me a Drum

Give me a drum to march by
That never misses a beat,
That leads me through the fog of doubt
And fires weary feet.

Offer me faith that laughs at fear
No matter who may scorn
And I will fight the hate of man
Till love itself is born.

Show me a cause that asks for all
The courage I possess
And I will raise my banner high
And stop for nothing less.—*Charles A. Waugaman*

Personal Evangelism While Traveling

The late bishop Joseph Berry said, "I do not go on the railroad train without seeking out someone who gives me at least one opportunity to say a good word for Jesus Christ." We need men who have the passion of the propagandist, whose eyes are open, whose hand is outstretched, and whose whole being is concentrated on and consecrated to the business of reaching lost souls.

He related that he took the sleeper on one occasion from Los Angeles to Chicago. He noticed that a Christian Science woman was talking in desperate earnestness with all the passengers she could about her religion. Bishop Berry turned to his wife and said, "My dear, that woman makes me feel very uncomfortable. I feel condemned, for every minute when she is not asleep she is working on this train for her special religion."

That night he took a walk through the train and he said to the porter, "Do you have anyone sick on this pullman?"

He said, "Yes, boss, we have a sick boy in there. Been sick ever since we left the coast." "Has anybody been in to talk with him?"

"Nobody but me, sir," said the porter. So Berry went in to see this lonesome lad. He was about twenty, with deeply sunken eyes. On his cheeks was the crimson glow of advanced tuberculosis.

"I told him that I did not know that he had been sick, so I tried to cheer him up with a couple of funny stories. I started to walk away, thinking that I had done the right thing; but as I reached the door of the pullman, I stopped as though I had been shot and thought to myself, *I wonder what the Christian Science woman would do if she were here with this boy.* Then I turned around and, with a prayer on my lips that God would guide me, went back and parted the curtain again. 'Well,' I said, 'I came back sooner than I expected. You said you were lonesome, and I forgot to tell you about a friend of mine who will come here and stay with you all night. He will never leave you if you will let him stay.' Then I preached Jesus to him, and he listened with wide-open eyes.

He asked, 'Do you think I will last long enough to get home? I telegraphed my mother, and she will be down to the train to meet me, but I have been feeling all day that I will not last until I get home.' So I offered to say a prayer with him in his berth. I got up and closed the curtain behind me and prayed with him. When I opened my eyes after praying, his eyes seemed to be so eager, so hungry. This Savior had become sweet and precious to him.

"I got up early the next morning and parted the curtain and looked in. It was not necessary for anyone to tell me that Jesus had been there in that berth. I said, 'Well, I guess everything is all right this morning.' 'Yes, everything is all right this morning,' he said. 'Why, you hadn't gone five minutes last night before he came, and I have been so happy all night I could hardly sleep. I'm glad you came early so I could tell you about it.'

"He got to Chicago, and I gave him to his mother. Before we parted, however, he took my hand and said something to me that seems too sacred to repeat. I have never forgotten that lesson on the railroad train. We all need the passion of personal evangelism. Oh, that we might catch the fire of it."

Dr. R. E. Speer's Story of the Conversion of His Boy

I carry around all the time a little card, which is one of my most precious possessions. A few weeks ago, when I got home one day after having been off, my little seven-year-old boy climbed up on my knee and gave me that card. He said, "Father, I am going to read you this card, and then I will tell you how I got it." So he began to read this simple little boyish card:

> God wants the boys, God wants the boys,
> The little boys, the noisy boys,
> The funny boys, the thoughtless boys,
> God wants the boys with all their joys,
> That he as gold may make them pure
> And teach them trials to endure.
> His heroes brave he would have them be,
> Fighting for truth and purity.
> God wants the boys.

And he said: "I will read you the other side: 'Are you willing to be God's boy? If so, sign your name to this covenant and daily ask God to help you keep it: I receive Jesus as my Savior, and I will try hard to do what I think he would have me do.' Now I will tell you how I got it," he said. "Randolph Sailer and I were playing the other day in the new barn that they are building just over there, and we sat down and talked together about the Bible. One of the carpenters heard us, and he came over and sat down beside us. He talked to us, and then he said: 'Boys, I've got some cards I want to give you.' Then he went over where his coat was hanging beside his dinner pail, and he got the cards like this out of his pocket. He gave one of them to me and one to Randolph."

This man was not educated in the finest colleges, but he knew what it was to live the full life. He was not willing to spend his life out sawing timber and hammering nails any more than a man ought to be willing to spend his life out pleading causes in court or patching up the bodies that are the houses in which we live. I tell you, fellows, we are not our bodies; we are lives. We were put into this world not to give our bodies a little sensual pleasure or to furnish them a little mental work. We were put into this world to live with our lives for the life of men. Have you begun to live that way yet? The man who is going out, sent of God, into the world is going to live his life for life; and after his life is gone, his life is what he will have forever.

How Lorimer Was Led

Dwight L. Moody, America's greatest evangelist, was led to Christ by a Sunday School teacher, Mr. Kimberly, in the rear of a shoe store on Court Street in Boston. Dr. George H. Lorimer, perhaps the most famous of the pastors of Tremont Temple, Boston, and whose son became editor of the *Saturday Evening Post*, began his career as a theatrical man. He was won to Christ in Louisville when some women went to their pastor, Dr. Everetts, and suggested that invitations to church service be passed out at neighborhood doors. The women passed an invitation card to George H. Lorimer; but he replied, "No, you haven't any use for me. I'm a theatrical man." The women were so courteous, however, that he could not refuse their invitation and came to church. Dr. Everetts' sermon was "The summer is ended, the harvest is passed, and I am not saved." Lorimer was saved in church that Sunday and later became pastor of Tremont Temple, Boston. One of the young lawyers who listened to his preaching was Russell H. Conwell. Lorimer led Conwell to accept Christ. Conwell went to Philadelphia and built the great Temple University and the Grace Baptist Temple there.

You Must Take Up the Cross

An American businessman went to Oberammergau to witness the famous passion play, just before the outbreak of World War II. Enthralled by this great drama that depicts the story of the cross, he went backstage at the conclusion of the play to meet Anton Lang, who played the part of the Christus. Our American friend had equipped himself with an expensive camera which he was eager to use. Abruptly he snapped the picture of Anton Lang, much to Mr. Lang's discomfort. Then looking about the stage for something more to shoot with his camera, he saw over in the corner the great cross that Mr. Lang had carried up the hill to Calvary in the play. Quickly turning to his wife, he said, "Here, dear, you take my camera. I'm going over and lift up the cross. When I get it up on my shoulder, you snap my picture carrying the cross. Won't that be a novel and exciting picture to send home to our friends in America?"

He saw that Mr. Lang was frowning severely at the brusque irreverence of the American tourist. "You don't mind, do you, Mr. Lang?" he said. "This is very unusual," protested Mr. Lang; but before he could say more, the man had hurried over beside the cross. He stooped down to lift it to his shoulder, but he could not budge it one inch off the floor—the cross was made of heavy iron oak beams.

Puffing with amazement, the man turned to Mr. Lang and said, "Why, I thought it would be light. I thought the cross was hollow. Why do you carry a cross that is so terribly heavy?"

Mr. Lang drew himself up to his full height and replied with compelling dignity and rebuke, "Sir, if I did not feel the weight of his cross, I could not play his part." Can the churches, can any man, can you?

Why We Miss the Christ

It was Sunday afternoon, and a little girl sat near her father, looking at a book of religious pictures while he read the newspaper. She stopped turning the pages as she came to a picture of a man dressed in kingly robes carrying a jeweled, lighted lantern in his hand and knocking at a door beside which grew thorns and bramble bushes. The door had been closed a long time, and briers had grown up about it.

The picture was Holman Hunt's famous painting *The Light of the World*. You will remember that the artist has placed no handle on the outside of the door, for the door of the soul must be opened from within.

Fascinated by the kind face of the man, the little girl was caught by the mystery and beauty of the portrait. She developed a rapport with the kingly figure knocking at the door. "Daddy," she said, "why don't the people let the nice man in when he knocks?"

Her father had told her never to disturb him at his reading and paid no attention.

Left alone with her problem, still silently contemplating the strong, patient face, she said again, "Why don't the people let the man in?"

Indifferent, her father met the question with a silent rebuff. This time the little girl was silent a long time, deeply immersed in her own thoughts. Suddenly she broke the silence with a ripple of laughter, as though she had discovered the answer.

She ran to her father and cried, "Oh, Daddy, now I know why the people don't let him in. The people in the house can't hear him because they are all *down cellar*."

Reconciliation and Salvation

The author of "This Is My Father's World" was Maltbie D. Babcock, a Presbyterian pastor in Brooklyn, New York. Democratic in spirit, he canceled the system of renting pews and opened all pews free to the public. But one wealthy woman in his church bitterly resented this new pew system, particularly when she found strangers in her pew on Sunday mornings. She left the church in hot indignation and vowed she would never speak to Dr. Babcock again.

In the spirit of reconciliation, like a wise pastor, Dr. Babcock called at the residence of the angered dowager. The maid answered the bell and said, "Mrs. Blank is not at home." He called again the next day and a pert maid announced, "Mrs. Blank is not at home today." Once more, on Wednesday, the pastor rang the bell at the big front door, only to have an insolent maid declare, "Mrs. Blank is never at home to Dr. Babcock." In dead earnest, Dr. Babcock returned on Thursday; and, like a good salesman, the instant the door was opened he put his foot in and entered the front hall, saying to the astonished maid, "Kindly tell Mrs. Blank that her pastor is waiting for her in her front parlor."

At this moment Mrs. Blank was in her upstairs living room with her husband and two daughters. She said to her husband, "You go down and dismiss him from this house, for I will never go down to see him if he stays there until the crack of doom!" In this family dilemma one of the daughters said to her agitated mother, "Just calm yourself, Mother. I'll go downstairs, and trust me to dismiss him quickly from the house." She tripped blithely down the stairs, not knowing the special charm Dr. Babcock had. He soon engaged this daughter with captive grace in conversation about her need of Christ. His persuasive appeal led her then and there to give her heart and life to Christ.

Meanwhile, upstairs, the mother grew more and more angry and mystified because Dr. Babcock had not left the house; nor had the daughter returned. Therefore, the second daughter said, "Mother, I'm going down to see what is wrong and why he doesn't leave."

When this daughter entered the room she was surprised to see the joy and glow on her sister's face. The pastor soon drew this daughter in the fascinating conversation and before long won her, also, to her confession of faith in Jesus as her Lord and Savior.

By now the mother was ready to burst. She could no longer restrain her temper. Wrenching open her door, she strode down the elegant staircase in a haughty spirit of bitterness, saying to herself, "I'll send that hateful pastor running from this house at the snap of my fingers!" As she entered her parlor, her head held high, Dr. Babcock came forward politely, with a glowing daughter on either arm, and said, "Mrs. Blank, may I present to you your two lovely daughters, never lovelier than now, for they have just accepted Jesus Christ as their Savior. I was about to kneel with your daughters as they dedicate their lives to him and his church. Wouldn't you like to kneel with them and give your own heart to Christ in a new way of forgiveness?"

The haughty woman melted in a moment and burst into tears. "Pastor," she cried, "I am a proud, bitter, and unreasonable woman with a haughty spirit. What do I really care about my church pew since you have brought my daughters to Christ—they are dearer to me than all the rest of the world!" The visit did not end until Dr. Babcock had the father, mother, and their two daughters on their knees with him in prayer. He made opposition an occasion of reconciliation, repentance, and salvation. Quarrels can be made into steps toward Christ when we are "wise as a serpent and harmless as a dove."

If Jesus Came to Your House

If Jesus came to your house to spend a day or two,
If he came unexpectedly, I wonder what you'd do.
Oh, I know you'd give your nicest room to such an honored guest,
And all the food you'd serve to him would be the very best,
And you would keep assuring him you're glad to have him there,
That serving him in your home is joy beyond compare.
But when you saw him coming, would you meet him at the door
With arms outstretched in welcome to your heav'nly visitor?
Or would you have to change your clothes before you let him in,
Or hide some magazines and put the Bible where they'd been?
Would you turn off the radio and hope he hadn't heard,
And wish you hadn't uttered that last, loud, hasty word?
Would you hide your worldly music and put some hymn books out?
Could you let Jesus walk right in, or would you rush about?
And I wonder, if the Savior spent a day or two with you,
Would you go right on doing the things you always do?
Would you keep right on saying the things you always say?
Would life for you continue as it does from day to day?
Would your family conversation keep up its usual pace,
And would you find it hard each meal to say a table grace?
Would you sing the songs you always sing and read the books you read,
And let him know the things on which your mind and spirit feed?
Would you take Jesus with you everywhere you'd planned to go,
Or would you, maybe, change your plans for just a day or so?
Would you be glad to have him meet your very closest friends,
Or would you hope they'd stay away until his visit ends?

Would you be glad to have him stay forever on and on,
Or would you sigh with great relief when he at last was gone?
It might be interesting to know the things that you would do,
If Jesus came in person to spend some time with you.

The Conversion of Henry W. Grady

In Atlanta, Georgia, there stands a monument to Henry W. Grady, leader of the New South, editor of the *Atlanta Constitution*, and eloquent orator. When the International Convention of the Y.M.C.A. met in Atlanta, the delegates clasped hands at the closing session of the convention and sang a Christian hymn. Grady refused to join hands and to sing the hymn. Grady said to the young men, "You notice that I could not join hands with you and sing that Christian hymn. You young men have something I do not have. Years ago in my old home in Athens with my dear mother, I used to have it. The hurly-burly and the business of the world have swept it out of my life. I want to get it back. Please tell me how to get it."

As best they could, the young men told him what Jesus meant to them. The next day this famous Southerner went to his office and told his associates that he would be away for a week and that he wished no one to know where he was going. "Don't worry," he said, "I shall report back here when I get ready." He took the first train to the home of his childhood. Reaching home, he said, "Mother, I have come to stay awhile. I want to go back to the old days and have you treat me just as you used to when I was a little boy. Make me some little pie-dough cakes and apple turnovers and some ginger horses with raisin eyes." In the quiet afternoons he would throw himself down on the couch and say, "Mother, tell me Bible stories as you used to, about Joseph and his coat of many colors, about David and his sling, and about Daniel and the lions."

Sometimes he would go to the table and bring the family Bible and say, "Mother, read me again the sweet story of the birth of Christ and of the angels who sang and ·· the Wise Men who followed the star. Read me how he went about doing good and how he suffered and died." When he would retire at night he would say, "Mother, come and hear me say my good night prayers." Then, as many great men before him have done, he prayed, "Now I lay me down to sleep. I pray the Lord my soul to keep."

Grady stayed for two weeks in his boyhood home with his mother. Something had happened in his life. He had found the fountain of life everlasting in his mother's religion. Returning to Atlanta, he found on his desk an invitation from the New England Society of New York City to be the annual speaker. He went and gave his great oration which thrilled the country from ocean to ocean, "The Old South and the New." It was the first time that the South had spoken eloquently since the Civil War, with a message of love and peace and hope and reconciliation.

Christian mothers are the greatest personal evangelists.

Living the Resurrection

If the Christian really believed in the resurrection, that belief would transform his daily living. This fact was brought vividly home to me the first time I attended a performance of Richard Wagner's opera "Die Walkure" in the New York Metropolitan Opera House. Jerome Hines sang Woton that night, and Anita Valkki, a Finnish soprano, debuted as Brunnhilde.

The final dialogue between father and daughter soars in rapturous tones over the thundering orchestral chords and the enveloping marvels of the strings, then dies in the pulsing melodies and the flaming stage impressions of the "Magic Fire Music" finale.

Something was electric in the performance, and one could feel the singers rising above and beyond their actual physical limitations. Knowing Mr. Hines personally, I hurried backstage to greet him, while the audience went wild with praise, demanding curtain call after curtain call. When Jerry finally came into the wings, he was radiant with an excitement that superseded mere delight in an audience's appreciation.

"As I sang that final scene tonight, for the first time I realized that Woton's words contain an argument for the resurrection," he told me, and he began to quote from the libretto. Here was the clue to a unique performance. Being a Christian, Jerry had caught a vision of his faith in the most unexpected of places, and it had inspired his creation of an operatic role. His enthusiasm had flamed through the other soloists and the orchestra to thunder forth in sheer triumph.

If every Christian were so inspired by the reality of Jesus' resurrection, we would soon flood the dark world around us with the brilliance of God's love.

5

God Our Father

God the Creator

Scholar, poet, essayist, and editor of the famous *Spectator,* Joseph Addison was at one time the most popular man in England. By his writings and influence he turned English literature away from licentiousness back to Christian morality and faith. One of his poems so entranced George Washington that the President declared it greater than all other poems.

Addison's great hymn for which Haydn provided the music, "The Spacious Firmament," contains lines that no atheist can gainsay.

> This spacious firmament on high
> With all the blue ethereal sky,
> And spangled heavens a shining frame
> Their Great Original proclaim,
> The unwearied sun from day to day
> Does his Creator's power display.
>
> What, though no real voice or sound,
> Amid the radiant orbs be found?
> In reason's ear they all rejoice,
> And utter forth the glorious voice
> Forever singing as they shine,
> The hand that made us is Divine.

God's Plan for Our Lives

God's plan for our lives often runs counter to our own desires and plans. Sometimes we cannot understand why God's plans for others seem to elevate them to honor and success, while his plans for us have led us into ways of suffering and humble service not regarded as honor or success.

In the third part of the *Divine Comedy* the great poet Dante explained this common problem with this story: There was a very religious woman, now in heaven, who realized that others had received greater honor and abundant joy beyond hers. At this point, Dante had someone ask, "Is this not a flaw in your happiness?" The answer she gave was a beautiful response that has comforted many souls through the centuries: "In his will is our peace." Once we believe this, there is no rebellion left, no envy, no complaint; it is indeed the only way to solve our problems—"In his will is our peace."

God's Hand

The American blacks placed the whole world in God's hand. The poet Maude Rubin worked her own variation on that picture.

> God holds us in his hand, as we hold pebbles,
> Blowing away the sand and dust of storm;
> He holds us to the light to note our luster—
> Then puts us to the wheel for finished form.

Discouragement Is Blind

F. W. Faber reverted to the unvisualized God in these lines.

> Oh, it is hard to work for God
> Upon this battlefield of earth,
> To rise and take his part
> And not sometimes lose heart.

> Thrice blessed is he to whom is given
> The instinct that can tell
> That God is on the field
> When he is most invisible.

God's First

Dr. George Buttrick tells a story of a saint knocking at the door of heaven. He hears feet inside coming, then a voice saying, "Who's there?"

"I, Lord," the saint answered. The footsteps moved away.

Then the saint knocked again, heard the footsteps coming, and the voice again saying, "Who's there?"

"I, Lord," again said the saint, and he heard the steps again going away.

A third time the saint knocked, heard steps coming, and sensed someone pausing in front of the door. "Who's there?" came the voice.

"Thou, Lord," breathed the saint, and the door swung open.

Turning Tragedy into Victory

Dr. Gordon H. Schroeder tells the story of a small boy who was sailing a little toy boat on a pond. The boat drifted beyond reach, and he began to cry. An older boy standing nearby saw what happened and began to throw rocks in the direction of the boat. This turn of events made the little boy cry all the louder until he realized that the rocks were not hitting and sinking the boat, but gently bringing it back toward the shore. The rocks hit the water a little beyond the boat, and the ripples that followed moved the boat closer to the boy. Most of us react negatively when stones are thrown our way; but if we are patient, we will soon realize that our trials may contain possibilities for good. God's purposes are not always apparent at the time of difficulty, but in everything God works for good. When we draw upon the spiritual resources that God makes available to us, we can turn an hour of tragedy into a glorious victory.

God—the Source of Inspiration

Franz Joseph Haydn, probably the greatest composer of his age, who left a rich legacy of oratorios and symphonies, was once asked where he obtained his musical inspirations and ideas. Simple in his lifelong Catholic faith, he answered, "Well, you see, I get up early, and as soon as I have dressed I go down on my knees and pray God that I may have another successful day. Then when I've had some breakfast, I sit down at the clavier and begin my search. But if I can't get on, I know that I must have forfeited God's grace by some fault of mine, and then I pray once more for grace."

One of his greatest works is *The Creation*, based on the account of the creation in Genesis in the Bible and John Milton's *Paradise Lost*. He had to be carried, due to illness, to the gala Vienna performance of *The Creation*. In a tremendous ovation the distinguished audience rose with thunderous applause as a tribute to his genius. Franz Haydn protested and, pointing his hand toward heaven, exclaimed, "This did not come from me—it all comes from above." Not only great music comes from inspiration by God; but how often in our daily work of life the Holy Spirit whispers to us, "This is the way; walk ye in it."

Green Lake's Dedicated Motto

"God made the country, but man made the cities," said the English poet and hymn writer William Cowper, himself a great lover of country life and ways. One thinks of this saying when one visits the beautiful American Baptist Assembly in Green Lake, Wisconsin, where groups from different denominations gather for summer conferences amid lakeside walks, rose gardens, and sylvan winding roads. It is "the country" indeed, in breathtaking glory and inspiring enchantment.

The assembly is dedicated to this purpose: "For a Closer Walk with God." This high theme was taken from one of Cowper's best-known hymns:

> O for a closer walk with God,
>   A calm and heavenly frame:
> A light to shine upon the road,
>   That leads me to the Lamb!

Shy and extremely nervous, Cowper had suffered a mental breakdown from holding to the obsession that he was a lost soul eternally damned. Recovering from his deep spiritual depression, he wrote another stanza to the hymn:

> Return, O holy Dove, return,
>   Sweet messenger of rest;
> I hate the sins that made thee mourn
>   And drove thee from my breast.

As the peace of God returned him to serenity of mind, he wrote the last stanza:

> So shall my walk be close with God,
>   Calm and serene my frame;
> So purer light shall mark the road
>   That leads me to the Lamb.

In his enormous depression Cowper tried suicide four times. He took poison, but it did not work. Then he went to the Thames River and jumped in, but was rescued. He rushed home and fell on a knife, but the blade broke. Finally he found a rope and hanged himself. Though unconscious, he was cut down just in time to save his life.

After this he came to a new and profound faith in God and wrote:

> God moves in a mysterious way
> His wonders to perform.

He plants his footsteps in the sea
And rides upon the storm.

Aftermath

Above the cloud, the star.
Sheathed in the bud, the flower.
Up through the crucible of grief
Comes insight's finest hour.

After the struggle, peace,
When we bend to kiss the rod.
After earth's turmoil and unrest,
The great beyond—and God!—*Jane Crowe Maxfield*

The Ignorance of God

Mark Twain's European travels proved to be a triumphal tour. All the notables of Europe invited him to dine with them. Once, on receiving an invitation from the emperor of Germany to come to the palace to dinner, Mark Twain's daughter, Susy, spoke up to her father. Sharing his pride, she said, "Daddy, you know most everybody in the whole world now, don't you, except God?" Of how many lives it can be said they know so much about so many things—except God.

Belief in God

Kepler, the astronomer, prayed, "Almighty God, these are thy thoughts that I am thinking after thee." Isaac Newton called God "the Geometrician." Professor Jeans calls God "the Mathematician." Eddington, the physicist, calls God "the Poet."

Herbert Spencer said, "The First Cause must be independent. It exists in the absence of other existence. It must be in every sense perfect, including within its own power and transcending all law. To use the established word, it must be Absolute."

E. Stanley Jones, a great Methodist leader, said, "God is the silent servant of us all. He is the great self-giver back of everything. Therefore, God is the ruler of us all."

Professor Brunner says, "God is the origin of reason and, therefore, is greater than reason. You can put reason into God, but you cannot put God into reason. God is the larger box. Therefore, you must add faith.

A God wholly comprehensible to reason would be no God because he would be no greater than our own reason. A God worthy of our worship must be beyond our reason."

Lord Bacon said, "I would rather believe all the fables in the legend and the Talmud and the Alcoran, than that this universal frame is without a mind . . . A little philosophy inclineth a man's mind to atheism, but depth in philosophy bringeth about a man's mind to religion."

E. Parks Cadman said, "For me God is that final reality through whom all else exists and without whom nothing else could be."

God's Healing Powers

Among God's miracles of healing must be included the plants and trees that yield healing medicines for our bodies.

The most beautiful tree in the whole world, say many naturalists, is an eighty-foot tall tree that grows on the sides of the Andes in Peru and Bolivia. Its large leaves are fiery red; its bark is yellow; and lilaclike flower clusters hang from its branches. The millions of sufferers of malaria over the world are grateful for the bark of this tree, which yields quinine, a specific cure for malaria. They are grateful for the Catholic missionaries who brought this curative bark to the physicians of the world. It is called the quina quina tree by the Indians, who first discovered its healing power.

In how many gardens the lavender flowers of the beautiful foxglove bloom in joy. All who suffer with heart disease are grateful that an old lady in Shropshire, England, made herb tea of the foxgloves' powdered leaves and cured sufferers of dropsy. In 1775 Dr. William Withering induced the old lady of Stafford to disclose her secrets. From the powdered leaves of the lavender and crimson flowering foxglove, he made digitalis. Digitalis not only aids the weakened heart; it also serves the ministry of healing with nine other medicinal benefits.

Or take the not-so-beautiful yam, which Dr. Russell Marker uncovered in Mexico and which he made yield, after years of laboratory research, hormones and steriods. In processing the humble yam Dr. Marker made it "into the finished drugs that help so many millions of patients," says Margaret Kreig in her book *Green Medicine*. In fact, many people today who are taking fertility-regulating pills have their destiny as parents rooted in the tropical wild yam. A miraculous substance from the organs of this plant is an essential element in the complex steroids that doctors give for family planning. Though they are sold under different trade names, the resulting products all start with the humble wild yam.

God's healing provisions for man are so abundant in nature that medical science has so far only scratched the surface of research and discovery. Everywhere God's miracles may be realized, for Jesus promised, "Seek, and ye shall find; knock, and it shall be opened unto you" (Matt. 7:7). These are but a few examples of God's marvelous goodness to the children of men. His fatherly benevolence to the just and the unjust alike should cause us to praise him, world without end.

The Faithfulness of God

The information we dutifully receive each day is not unlike that given in the black production *Green Pastures*. The angel Gabriel is sent down to investigate the havoc of Noah's flood. Returning, he gave his report: "Lord, there ain't nothing fastened down there anymore. Everything fastened down is coming loose." Well, it does seem that everything is coming loose, doesn't it? But don't you believe that either. The Ten Commandments, the Sermon on the Mount, the three angels' messages, and the love and faithfulness of God haven't budged an inch. God's unfailing Word says: "It is of the Lord's mercies that we are not consumed, because his compassions fail not. They are new every morning: great is thy faithfulness" (Lam. 3:22-23).

God Is Near

Many years ago I had a pastorate in northern Maine, where, on rare occasions, the temperature in January and February went as low as forty degrees below zero. If you have lived in those northern climes, you know that the frost gets into the beams of the houses and in the dead of night snaps with a bang and a boom, like a gun going off. It is a ghostly sound of frightening loneliness in the silence of the night.

On one of these winter nights my wife was away on a visit, and my little girl was sleeping alone in the room across the hall. She was awakened in the night by the booming of the frost in the beams of the house and cried from her room, in a frightened voice, to her father across the hall, "Daddy, are you there?" With an assuring voice I said, "Yes, Daddy is right here in his room."

Then in a few seconds there would be another boom and bang, shattering the silence with the eerie noise, and again I would hear her frightened, childish voice. "Daddy, are you there?" And I would reply in a voice as calm and assured as I could across the darkness, "Yes, darling, Daddy is right here near you, keeping watch all the time."

Then there would be a long silence. Once more there would be a bang and boom. And this time I took the initiative and said, "What is it that you want, dearie?" By this time, thrice assured that her father was there in the darkness, she recovered her calm of soul and piped up in a sweet, tiny voice of reply, "Oh, nothing! It's just a nice night, isn't it?"

So in all life's fearful, frightening experiences, once we have acquired faith that God our heavenly Father is keeping watch over his own, the unknown and the unexpected event loses its face of terror. Like a little child, we rest in the calmness of knowing that our Father is near.

6.
Jesus Christ the Lord

Christ the Center of History

Alexander MacLaren spoke of Christ as a midpoint in world history.

"Christ was placed midmost in the world's history; and in that central position, he towered like some vast mountain toward heaven—the farther slope stretching backward toward the creation, the thither slope toward the consummation of all things. The ages before looked to him with prophetic gaze; the ages since behold him by historic faith; by both he is seen in common as the brightness of the father's glory and as the unspeakable gift of God to the race.

"He stands alone in unapproachable grandeur. Nineteen centuries roll away and his character so lives that he inspires millions of men with impassioned love. He is the only one who can say in truth and holiness, 'Do as I have done.'"

Atheism Not Attractive

Clarence Darrow, famous trial lawyer, said, "The outstanding fact that cannot be dodged by thoughtful men is the futility of it all."

Bertrand Russell wrote about man, "His origin, his growth, his hopes, his fears, his loves, and beliefs are but the outcome of accidental collocations of atoms."

H. L. Mencken, iconoclast and atheist, wrote, "Life fundamentally is not worth living . . . What could be more logical than suicide? What could be more preposterous than keeping alive?"

Incarnation—Christmas

In one of E. Stanley Jones's speeches he related a long interview he had with the great Indian leader, Gandhi. Toward the end of the conversation Gandhi challenged Jones, "Tell me in one sentence what Christ means to you."

For a moment Stanley Jones quivered under the impact of the question and then reverently said, "All I want and need of God, that, Jesus Christ my Lord, is to me."

Christ Preeminent

good

When Leonardo da Vinci had completed his marvelous masterpiece "The Last Supper," it is said that he took an artist friend with him to inspect and criticize his work. The friend examined the masterpiece with great admiration, but his critical eye caught a flaw in the picture. He said to da Vinci, "You have painted the chalice on the table with exquisite beauty. It is the most beautiful thing in the whole picture and captivates the eyes of the beholder." Very deliberately da Vinci went to his palette, took his brush in his hand, and wiped out the superlatively beautiful chalice—the cup. He wanted nothing to take attention away from the face of Christ. "It is Christ who must be preeminently seen as the center of my painting," said the famous artist.

A hymn writer expressed the same thought when he wrote,

> The dearest idol I have known,
> What'er that idol be—
> Help me to tear it from thy throne
> And worship only Thee.

The Will to Good Comes by Grace

Thomas Carlyle, the gruff Scottish philosopher of great fame, had little use for preachers and the hard doctrines of Scotland's Presbyterianism. He liked to attack the church and her ministers.

One evening he was sitting in his mother's home by the warm fireside when the conversation revolved around preachers. "If I ever had to preach," said the surly Carlyle, "I would make short work of it. I would go into the pulpit and say no more than just this: Now all you people already know what you ought to do; well, now then, go on home and do it.' "

His aged mother, who was knitting in her rocking chair, put down her needles and, looking sharply at her son, said, "All right, Thomas, and then will you tell them how?" That stumped Carlyle.

Unless the will is redeemed by the grace of Christ, man is bereft of the inspiring motive and the enduring power to give himself unselfishly to the service of others. Knowledge of what is right, taken by itself, will not save us. The will to do the right at any cost comes from the crucified Lord of Calvary.

An Example of Character

A flower of American manhood was Gen. Robert E. Lee. Although generally conceded to have been the greatest general on either side of the War Between the States, he was at the same time a self-controlled Christian gentleman. Though relatively a short man, his stature stands tall and towering among Americans.

A Virginian by birth and loyalty, he was something of a Puritan, too. He did not smoke or drink or gamble, and he was regular in his church attendance. When revivals swept the army of northern Virginia he attended them with his soldiers. Personally he kept no slaves. The army life he was forced to live, even with a heart disease, did not corrupt him. He had no mistress, and he was not a woman chaser. He was a God-fearing man.

Unlike so many leaders of our day, General Lee shines with unfading luster as a man of integrity, loyalty, and honor. He had fervent loyalty for his country as he understood it. He holds a place of supreme admiration in our nation's history—a most worthy example for men of our day to follow.

Do We Care?

One of the saddest stories I know came some years ago from the personal confession of a veteran missionary.

This man had spent forty years in an Oriental country, where he suffered every type of deprivation, isolation, and hardship for Christ's sake. His field was a lonely mission station surrounded by backward natives, and he often yearned for the fellowship of Christian believers. But after forty years, when he was broken in health, the time had come for him to say a final farewell and return to America. He had served his denomination well.

By coincidence he returned to New York on the same ship on which Teddy Roosevelt was a passenger. Teddy was returning from a brief hunting trip in Africa. As the great ocean liner docked, there on the wharf was a great crowd. Most of the crowd was dressed in cowboy hats, shirts, and scarves, carrying flags. "Welcome home, Teddy," they shouted, and there was a band, too. Also on the dock were several smaller delegations who welcomed special friends or members of their families. Our missionary suddenly thought, *I must search for some of my brethren who have come to welcome me, too*, and his eyes roamed the crowds as he stood on the ship's deck. *Surely*, he thought, *someone will be here, for forty years is a long time to be away*. But his heart sank. No one—not a single soul from his denomination, which he had served so faithfully, was there to grasp his hand or to say, "Welcome home!"

In his hotel room in New York that night, he sank into loneliness and despondency. (No place is more depressing than a New York hotel room!) In his utter discouragement he said to himself, *Was it worth it all? Who cares?* His faith almost went "on the rocks." Finally, as all good Christians do, he went to his Bible for comfort and prayed to Jesus to give him back the joy and peace he had lost.

This man's experience raises questions: Do we honor those who have worn themselves out in the service of our Lord? Do we neglect or forget them? How many souls around us need a pat on the shoulder or a word of praise or gratitude? Jesus said, "Ye . . . visited me" (Matt. 25:36). The cheer we give to lonely souls is given, indeed, to Jesus himself.

The Necessity of Roots

Many of our churches seem full of shallow Christians of superficial faith. Jesus described those who withered away under the scorching sun "because they had not root" (Matt. 13:6). Paul said we can only know the love of Christ by "being rooted and grounded in love" (Eph. 3:17).

Neither can plants exist without strong and even elaborate root systems, as Jesus indicated.

At the University of Iowa, a graduate student, now Professor Howard J. Dittmer, Professor of Biology and Dean of the Graduate School of New Mexico University, made a laboratory study of a single rye plant. The experiment was carefully conducted, writes Professor Robert L. Hulbary of Iowa University, and special procedures were used in measuring the system of roots of the single rye plant. The results of the measurement estimates are not only astonishing; they seem incredible, should one not know nature's insistence and dependence on wide and deep roots. The scientific laboratory experiment measured 378 miles of roots supporting this single rye plant. Imagine! The plant put out 143 main roots from which it expanded secondary, tertiary, and quaternary roots. The microscopic root hairs ran into millions in the count.

If a single plant could not grow without 378 miles of roots, how can Christians grow in grace and spiritual fruitfulness without putting down deep roots in Bible study, in the habit of prayer, in loyalty to the church, in service for Christ, in fidelity in stewardship, in good works that glorify God?

The Vital Power of Roots

A famous scientist, Dr.Loren Eiseley, Professor of the History of Science at the University of Pennsylvania, in his book *The Unexpected Universe* (New York: Harcourt, Brace and World, Inc., 1969) writes as if roots have willpower.

He says, "A kind of desperate will resides even in a root. It will perform the evasive tactics of an army slowly inching its way through crevices and hoarding energy until some day it swells and a living tree upheaves the heaviest mausoleum. I have seen a tree root burst a rock face on a mountain or slowly wrench aside the gateway of a forgotten city. This is a very cunning feat which men take too readily for granted."

The Spreading of the Word of God

Quietly but steadily the Word of God is being spread by translation into many new languages and dialects. Organized to promote translations of the Bible in all parts of the world, even among remote tribes, are the scholarly and dedicated Wycliffe Bible translators. Founded by Dr. William Cameron Townsend, the Wycliffe translators have completed in recent years translations of the Scriptures into nine hundred languages. Dr. Townsend points out that there are two thousand languages left, representing 200,000,000 people who do not even have small portions of the Bible in their own tongue. The Wycliffe translators have set a target date of the year 2000 to complete the translation of the Bible in the two thousand remaining languages.

Christ's Courtesy to Children

So often, like Christ's disciples, we do not fathom the depth of his courtesy. Good men that they were, they had no conception of his courtesy to children. In this respect they were men of their own generation, and Christ was giving the world an original virtue—the planting of a new flower in the desert. Compare, if you will, the loftiest of pagan philosophers with the Great Teacher. A professor chilled my blood once by asserting that Epictetus was greater than Christ. Well, I cease to become excited now over new messiahs. Epictetus did not like children, so mothers would not have brought their babies to him. Bachelors, he asserted, are greater benefactors to mankind than parents; and he referred to children as "evilly-squalling brats." When Socrates' own children were brought to his cell on his last day to live, he ordered them away because they disturbed his philosophical conversation.

Jesus' Use of Humor

Dr. T. R. Glover, Baptist scholar and teacher, points out our Lord's use of semihumorous imagination in his description of the Pharisees. Jesus said that the Pharisee polishes the cup elaborately and carefully on the outside, but forgets to clean the inside of the cup. Most people drink from the inside, but the Pharisee ignores this and leaves the cup dirty. But he then sets about straining what he is going to drink. The Pharisee must be so exact. With an elaborate process he holds a piece of muslin over the top of the cup and pours with care—he pauses; alas, he sees a mosquito, catches it, and then flicks it away. He will not swallow that gnat—no, not on his life! But he turns right around and swallows a camel. The illustration is really a series of pictures. First he gulps the homely head; then the long, hairy neck slides down the throat of the Pharisee; the loose-hung anatomy, the humps, the knees, the spindly legs, the parted feet—all plug and choke the throat of the Pharisee, who is never really aware of how much he swallows. The picture was intended to make one laugh. A little laughter in a lesson never hurts. It, too, is a divine gift.

They Didn't Hang Him Very High

They didn't hang him very high,
Just high enough, I think,
That one tall man could offer him
Some vinegar to drink.

He didn't hang so *very* high,
Just high enough to view
The words that trembled on his lips:
"They know not what they do."

And yet he hung so very high—
Higher than scepter, orb, or crown—

He reached from earth up to the sky
And brought us heaven down,
And brought us heaven down!—*Bertie Cole Bays*

Death Not Beautiful

I was riding along in a Cadillac with a wealthy and prosperous businessman of about sixty years of age. We passed slowly by one of the most beautiful cemeteries in America. I waved my hand and said, "Isn't that the most beautiful cemetery you ever saw?" There were magnificent beds of blooming flowers in well-groomed designs; a variety of trees from cypress to weeping willows lined the roads and paths; the lawns were green and neatly trimmed; white marble mausoleums were scattered through the park as well as impressive monuments and statues. To my amazement, my friend answered my remark with a vociferous and savage voice. "No, to me every cemetery is ugly and hateful. I despise all cemeteries." Then, softening his angry tone a bit, he said with pathos, "Do you know, I wish I could go to some country where there are no cemeteries." Well, do we not all have moments when we long for that better country where death never comes?

Obedience

Lord, as you hung upon the cross,
Men mocked and cried:
"Others he saved! Himself he cannot save!"
But O, my Lord, they lied!

The same authoritative voice that said:
"Let there be light!"
That sent the first bird winging on its flight;
That formed man, and the woman from his side;
That bade the seas obey the changing tide;
Could easily have loosed thee from the cross
And poured for us the vinegar of loss.

Nails never held thee!
Even less, did man.
Obedience bound thee to the Father's plan.
O cruel jest: that, had Thou so complied,
Thy mockers were, forever, crucified.—*Kathryn T. Galloway*

Proof of God's Love

There is the story of an eloquent monk in the Middle Ages who came to one of the cities of Europe and announced that the next day he would preach on the love of God.

The cathedral was crowded with a great congregation on the next day, breathlessly waiting to hear the great sermon that the monk had announced he would preach.

As the congregation waited, the rear door of the cathedral opened quietly; and the monk walked down the long aisle, bearing a lighted taper. Slowly he walked to the altar; but instead of ascending the pulpit, he stood before the crucifix, the large figure of Christ hanging on the cross.

In the awesome silence and without a word of comment, he held the lighted candle to the wounds in Christ's feet made by the spikes; then he lifted the candle to each nail print and the wound in each hand. Lastly, he held the lighted taper at Christ's side, where the spear had cut a deep wound. Then he blew out the candle and walked silently out of the cathedral.

This was his sermon on the love of God.

The Death of Christ

Help me to see in those I meet,
On country road or city street,
Not just strange people passing by
But those for whom Christ came to die.

Then through his eyes of love and grace
Let me find beauty in each face.
Those weary people passing by
Are those for whom Christ came to die.—*Anonymous*

The Present Power of the Cross

One Christian man in England, Professor George Turell, who faced great hostility from other Christians because of his own personal search for truth, wrote these words in the process of the conflict: "Again and again I have been tempted to give up the struggle, but always the figure of that strange man hanging on the cross sends me back to my tasks again."

The Face of Christ

Has any master painter truly depicted the face of Christ?

The world-famous *Pieta*, the work of the sculptor Michelangelo, was executed when he was a young man. It is regarded as one of the most lovely and perfect carvings of the face of Christ. This famous work was brought from Rome to New York for exhibit so that thousands might view it with admiration.

But many people do not know that Michelangelo did four versions of the *Pieta*. The last (*Rondanini*) he executed in his old age. Those who see it observe with amazement that he never finished the carving of the face of Christ. They wonder why. The answer is that with the long years of experience as a Christian believer and with the growing wisdom of old age, he realized that such beauty and grace, such loveliness and power were in the face of Jesus that to express that matchless face defied all his masterly skills. It was left incomplete not because he did not have his former skills or was short of time, but because at last he knew that the face of Christ was beyond expression.

Strength in Christ

In World War I an officer was leading a company of British soldiers back to the front after they had been on furlough. It was raining; the road was muddy; and the countryside was war-scarred and desolate. The men knew that they were returning to possible death. Their shoulders sagged, and none spoke or sang. As they marched along, the officer glanced through the door of a ruined church and saw the figure of Christ on the cross. It suddenly brought him courage and hope.

Turning to his men, he gave the command: "Eyes, right! March!" The depressed and discouraged soldiers saw what he had seen; and in the suffering but triumphant Christ they found new strength and hope. They lifted their heads, squared their shoulders, and bravely marched forward.

Immortality—Easter

The stars shine over the earth;
The stars shine over the sea;
The stars look up to the mighty God;
The stars look down on me.

The stars have lived for a million years,

For a million years and a day;
But Christ and I shall live and love
When the stars have passed away.—*Anonymous*

Avoiding Mention of Christ

George Santayana of Harvard fame delineates how a well-known Unitarian minister grappled with Easter. He found a way by which he "might prudently avoid all mention of Christ." Instead, he might "blandly describe the resurrection of nature in the spring," followed by a compliment to science in its resurrection of new forces in the modern world, and wind up by discussing the "resurrection of heroic freedom in the American character."

This incident is matched by a Good Friday noonday service led by a well-known preacher, attended by the writer, in which the name of Jesus and his death were never alluded to, but the character of Calvin Coolidge was contemplated with overgenerous praise.

The Resurrection

In the famous Dreyfus trial that shook all France and became world famous, Zola, the lawyer defending Dreyfus, found himself facing a hostile judge. Zola was not allowed to present his defense witnesses or to refute the false testimony given against his client Dreyfus.

"The case is closed!" shouted the judge. Zola rose in protest and, pointing to a mural behind the judge—a painting of the crucifixion—exclaimed, "There was also a case once called a 'closed case.' "

The authorities thought that Jesus' case was closed. The Romans sealed the tomb and left a guard of soldiers before the door of the tomb. The Sanhedrin, who had asked for the guard of soldiers, thought with the Romans that the case was closed.

But no case is ever closed until God closes it. The power of God declared the open door of the tomb and declared that the crucifixion of Christ vindicated by his resurrection was but the beginning of a new age of the fulfillment of God's eternal victory.

Broken Seals

"A miracle!" men cried, when Christ broke through the seal
Upon his tomb.
"A miracle!" when through locked doors he gained

The upper room.
"A miracle!" I cry, "Still unsurpassed;
That through the hardness of my heart
He passed."—*Kathryn T. Galloway*

Decision for Christ

"You must wager. It is not optional . . . Let us weigh the gain and
the loss in wagering that God is."—*Blaise Pascal*

G. A. Studdert Kennedy in his poem "Faith" from his book *Unutterable
Beauty* wrote:

How do I know that God is good? I don't.
I gamble like a man. I bet my life
Upon one side in life's great war. I must;
I can't stand out. I must take sides.
The man who is neutral in this fight is not a man.
He's bulk and body without breath.

You want to argue? Well,
I can't. It is a choice. I choose the Christ.

An anonymous poet wrote,

I'd rather walk with God by faith
Than to walk alone by sight;
I had rather walk with God in the dark
Than to walk alone in the light.

With Christ

Sir Robert Stopford was commander of one of the ships that Nelson
used to chase a fleet nearly double the size of his own to the West Indies.
Describing the experiences and hardships of that desperate adventure,
Stopford wrote these words in a letter: "We are half-starved, and otherwise
inconvenienced by being so long out of port. But our reward is that we
are with Nelson!"

Life may prove harsh and difficult. Your dreams may have faded, and
you may have run into troublesome times; but if you can say, "I am
with Christ, and through Christ with God," there is still hope. You can

count on God to help you turn difficult situations into spiritual opportunities.

Napoleon's Tribute to Christ

Napoleon, in exile in St. Helena, wrote, "I know men, and I tell you that Jesus Christ is not a man. Superficial minds have set a resemblance between Christ and the founders of empires and the gods of other religions. That resemblance does not exist. There is between Christianity and whatever other religions the distance of infinity.

"Everything in Christ astonishes me. His spirit overawes me, and his will confounds me. Between him and whoever else in the world there is no possible term of comparison. He is truly a being by himself. His ideas and his sentiments, the truths which he announced, his manner of convincing are not explained by human organization nor by the nature of things."

Christ the Center of History

Ruskin asserted that no landscape, however beautiful, is true art unless the scene is touched with human life. The sea is a vast loneliness without a distant white sail, and the mountains are forbidding without the genial roof of the Alpine shepherd's home.

In a similar way, if we view history as a great landscape, Jesus becomes necessary to its beauty and meaning. Human history that does not mention Christ leaves the world an immense canvas, desolate with meaninglessness. Christ is the truth necessary to give point and purpose to the painting of history's panorama. The biblical revelation is a movement pulsating in the heart of history. "History is 'His Story,'" wrote Pierson, "if one climbs high enough to read it."

From an Unbiased Observer—Tribute to Christ

George Bernard Shaw, the Irish playwright who lived to be more than ninety years of age, wrote: "The only person who has come out of the war with new intellectual credit is Jesus Christ . . . I am not a Christian any more than Pilate was, but I am ready to admit after studying the world of human misery for many years that I see no way out of the world's trouble but the way Jesus would have found had he undertaken the work of the modern practical statesman."

7.
The Holy Spirit

The Power of the Holy Spirit

Perhaps we need once more to surrender our stressful efforts to the tides of the Spirit of God. A ship may lose its way, confused by the dense fog, until it hits a reef and lies stranded at low tide. Immediately a dozen great tugs, belching black smoke and fire, rush to the rescue. Hausers are thrown to the big liner. The fierce engines of the tugs churn the waters into white mountains of foam, pulling and straining in vain. The ropes break—the ship is not budging one inch from where it is stuck fast.

Then the captain bids the tugs turn aside. He decides to rely on an almost unseen power. He waits with patience for the flooding in of the tide. Through the hours, silently surging higher, inch by inch, the rising water moves in; and the ship floats off the reef, uplifted by the irresistible tide.

So it is when we are upborne by the Spirit of God. The difficult becomes possible, and the impossible gets done.

Without a Pentecost

As long as pilgrims of this earth
Can turn from wars and things
To celebrate a baby's birth
And know the joy he brings;
As long as through the halls of death
Where grieving millions grope,
Men catch the glad, victorious breath
Of Easter's shining hope;
Let men recall an upper room,
Warm hearts and eager feet
That sped to light a world of gloom.
The news they bore, how sweet!

Would Christmas, Easter, not be lost
Indeed, without a Pentecost?—*Berniece Ayers Hall*

God's Holy Spirit Seeks Us

A hymn by an unknown writer says:

> I sought the Lord and afterward I knew,
> He moved my soul to seek him, seeking me.
> It was not I that found O Savior true;
> No, I was found of thee.
> I find, I walk, I love, but O the whole
> Of love is but my answer, Lord, to thee
> For thou wert long beforehand with my soul.
> Always thou lovedst me.

The Holy Spirit, the Agent of the Love of God

Early in my ministry, I was guest preacher on a summer's day in one of those beautiful white colonial New England churches. "The Love of God" was my theme. What I said was all true and probably helpful, yet inadequate. Something was lacking. After the service, as I walked away from the church, I was joined by a much older layman. I knew of him as a man of limited formal education, but he possessed a knowledge of the Scriptures that would put most ministers to shame. He had a kind comment on my sermon and then, without offense, revealed what I had not grasped before. "How wonderful," he exclaimed, "that Paul in Romans 5:5 tells us that this tremendous 'love of God is shed abroad in our hearts by the Holy Spirit.' Moffatt's translation," he added, "makes it even clearer. 'God's love floods our hearts through the holy Spirit.'" He paused and said, "Andrew Murray always said that this flooding of love into our hearts 'is the first work of the Holy Spirit.'"

That day I understood why some persons convey to us the love of God by their abounding joy, their active compassion, and their warm fellowship. They are literally *flooded* (NEB) by the love of God. To them this love is not a remote theological concept, but an activity inspired by genuine feeling. I prayed that such a flood of love might overflow from my heart to all I meet and touch.

The Holy Spirit as Wind

What does wind do?

1. It *sings!* Does he work through our hymn singing of joy?
2. It *cleanses* the air of pollution. How fresh the air we breathe when the wind blows away the foul air!
3. It *powerfully drives.* The Holy Spirit is driving power—watch the sailboats—it is power to witness.
4. It *creates patterns of beauty*—on the sand, on the sea, on the lake, on the smallest puddle.
5. It *invigorates the person.* After a stagnation of air, how fresh winds stir up our latent powers to activity—as the sea is stirred to vast emotion by the wind.
6. Jesus referred to the Holy Spirit as "the wind." At Pentecost there was the sound of a "great rushing wind."

Ten References to the Holy Spirit in Ephesians

1. Be filled with the Spirit.
2. Sealed with the Holy Spirit (1:13-14).
3. Access in one Spirit to the Father (2:18).
4. Habitation of God in the Spirit (2:22).
5. Strengthen with power through his Spirit (3:16).
6. Diligence to keep the unity of the Spirit in bond of peace (4:3).
7. Grieve not the Spirit in whom ye are sealed (4:30).
8. Not drunk but filled with the Spirit (5:18).
9. Take the sword of the Spirit (6:17).
10. Praying at all seasons in the Spirit (6:18).

The Fellowship of the Holy Spirit Makes a Difference

A friend of mine went to a Sunday worship service where everything was in excellent taste—but icily correct and precise in timing, music, sermon, and architecture. Service for this all-white congregation of prosperous upper middle-class persons ended on the dot of the hour. Everyone filed out stiffly without smiles, handshakes, or nods, apparently cautious lest the veneer of sanctity be cracked. When my friend got outside the church, the warmth and brotherly friendliness of the sunshine cured him of his chill.

On another Sunday he was invited to a different church. The styles of dress were far less fashionable. The congregation, not completely white, included a large segment of youth and many family groups. The architecture was probably second-rate. Actually he had hardly noticed the building because the congregation was glowing with gladness, and individually the people were relaxed and ardently friendly. Indeed, a spirit of love pervaded the church with great warmth. The hymns were sung with fervor by all. The worship service surrendered to spontaneity and relaxation rather than to precision and nicety. My friend came away from the service having met or made perhaps a dozen new friends. The sunshine seemed less important at the moment because he had experienced the exhilaration of a warm, gladdening power. He realized that he had seen and felt the Holy Spirit at work, creating fellowship. Now he understood the early Christian benediction, "The grace of the Lord Jesus Christ, and the love of God, and *fellowship* in the *Holy Spirit,* be with you all" (2 Cor. 13:14, NEB).

The Holy Spirit—the Wind of God

Standing along the California high shore land, one watches a yacht, whose contour is as graceful as a bird's, riding at anchor in the bay. The smoothly shaped boat is distinguished by a ninety-foot mast, fastened to which an enormous white canvas sail is hoisted. Now suddenly one sees the yacht driving forward with amazing speed, cutting through the mighty waves of the great Pacific Ocean. One wonders at this strong force that drives the ship with beauteous grace through all the resisting waves. There is no engine, no motor, no turbine, no engineering machinery. Only invisible power.

Following like a flock of sea gulls, a hundred small yachts with red, white, orange, and blue sails put out to sea, racing out into the surging waves, a picture of glory in the sun shining upon the blue waters. Strangely enough, not one of them has a motor either; yet they are driven forward and about in fast motion. The sight of all these ships driving toward the far horizon is beautiful to behold! But how can there be power if our physical eyes cannot see it? The driving force of the mighty wind eludes our physical vision, veiled in its own unique invisibility.

One stands upon the shores of history watching twelve fishermen sail out to turn the world upside down. They have no natural endowment of power or any inherent force of genius; what blowing wind of God pushes their frail craft forward on a mighty mission?

From the shore of the Mediterranean one sees another vessel put out to sea with Paul at the helm. What drives this man to the ends of the earth through imprisonments, riots, beatings, hunger, persecutions, and shipwreck? He is often stricken with malaria and often attacked by robbers. What dynamic, driving wind pushes him on?

Fifteen centuries later, a monk, the son of a miner, gets into his frail craft and hoists his sail to truth and reform amid the most tempestuous seas. The driving wind carries him bravely forward to a great triumph for God.

Who pushed John Wesley, delicate man that he was, from end to end of England? Through riots, threats on his life, dangers of winter weather, and endless opposition, what force propelled him to his glorious mission?

Look around today. You discern men and movements of God driving forward as more light breaks forth from God's Holy Word. What today drives the church forward to a new surge of evangelism, a new drive toward greater unity, the new spiritual search of youth, a new concern for the hungry and oppressed, a new fellowship of love between Catholics and Protestants, and a score more signs that some spiritual force of great power is at work in the world?

The answer lies in Pentecost, "the birthday of the Holy Spirit." Pentecost came, said Luke in Acts 2:2, with a noise "of a strong driving wind" (NEB). Of this Holy Spirit Jesus told Nicodemus, "The wind blows where it will" (John 3:8, NEB). The winds of God's Holy Spirit are blowing in our day. We have but to put up sails that surrender to his wind to know the power at our back, pushing us forward to some new work for Christ our Lord.

The Holy Spirit's Candelabrum

The Holy Spirit in our hearts bears the fruit of the Spirit. We sing, "Holy Spirit, Light divine, Shine upon this heart of mine." We may visualize this by placing on the pulpit a candelabrum for nine candles.

We light the *candle of love*. It is the greatest and therefore the central candle.

Joy is the second candle we light, for the kingdom of heaven is joy, that our joy may be full.

Peace is the third candle—a special, priceless peace—"My peace I give you" (John 14:27).

Next we light the *candle of patience.* "Let us run with patience the race set before us" (Heb. 12:1).

Kindness is a beautiful light of the spirit—"brotherly kindness," Peter wrote (2 Pet. 1:7).

Next we light the *candle of goodness.* "Barnabas . . . was a good man and full of the Holy Ghost and of faith" (Acts 11:24).

Faithfulness is a bright shining candle. "Be thou faithful unto death, and I will give thee a crown of life" (Rev. 2:10).

The *gentleness candle* shines next to faithfulness. Paul wrote, "The servant of the Lord must be gentle" (2 Tim. 2:24).

The *candle of temperance* or self-control is the ninth candle. "Let your moderation be known to all men," Paul admonished (Phil. 4:5).

The fullness of the fruit of the Spirit sets the candelabrum a blazing glow of light.

Just so beautiful is a life in which the fruit of the Spirit shines. But in some lives, how many candles are unlighted!

Note: This can make a meaningful service with children on Pentecost in lieu of the children's sermon. A circle of candlesticks, with the tallest in the back center, can be used instead of a candelabrum. The following verses for each fruit of the Spirit can be read by children, thus involving them in the presentation: 1. *Love,* John 3:16; 2. *Joy,* John 15:11; 3. *Peace,* John 14:27; 4. *Patience,* Hebrews 12:1-2a; 5. *Kindness,* 2 Peter 1:7; 6. *Goodness,* Acts 11:24; 7. *Faithfulness;* Revelation 2:10; 8. *Gentleness,* 2 Timothy 2:24; 9. *Temperance,* Philippians 4:5.

Witnessing Not in Vain

Dr. Louis A. Evans, Jr., tells of a sixteen-year-old girl in high school who sat next to a brilliant young attorney in an evangelistic service. When the invitation to accept Christ was given, the girl summoned all her courage and said to the lawyer, "Sir, have you found Jesus?" In smart repartee he answered, "I didn't know that Jesus was lost!" (Thoreau answered once in much the same vein when he replied to one who asked him if he wanted to be reconciled to God, "I didn't know that God and I had ever had a quarrel.")

Seventeen years later in a far city, that attorney, then a judge on the State Supreme Court, joined the church. "I have never gotten away from the question that young girl asked me years ago," he said, "and I wish now I could tell her that I have found Jesus as my Savior."

Taking the Pilot on Board

It is always a thrilling moment when a great ocean liner's engines cease their vibration and the passengers rush to the deck to see a sloop or motorboat coming close to the big ship. Up the perpendicular ladder of the great ship climbs the pilot. The officer of the deck welcomes him as though he were the owner of the line. He is received by the captain as though he were the admiral himself. Then he stands on the bridge. The engines revolve again, and the ship moves into the harbor. It is a great moment in a ship's voyage. The pilot alone knows the safe course into the home port.

It is the biggest moment in any life when Christ the "pilot" is taken on board and allowed to put his hand on the helm of the soul. From that point on he commands and controls; and the soul can say with Paul, "It is no longer I who live, but Christ who lives in me."

8.
The Church

The Church and the Power of Christ

It was the first time he had ever covered a war, and the intense excitement struck terror to his soul. Ben Robertson, American correspondent, arrived in London on a Saturday night in the midst of the very worst air raids. Bombs were falling by the scores all over London. Fires were breaking out everywhere. Walls were shattered, crumbling into heaps of ruins. Fire-engine sirens were sounding, and engines were dashing through the streets. There were the agonies and cries of the wounded and dying. Robertson said that for ten miles all around London there was just one huge circle of red flame. It was as if all hell had broken loose.

Finally, when the all-clear alert sounded at one o'clock in the morning, Robertson dragged himself back to the hotel. He said he was so nervous and exhausted that he could only fling himself on his bed and cry out to God, "Oh, God, I don't want to live another day. I can't go through another night of hell and horror like this. If this is what modern civilization has brought us to—if this is the best that modern man can achieve, then let me die in my sleep tonight. I don't want to wake again on earth and find myself in this hell." He said he finally fell asleep, but he did wake up in the morning; and he discovered that he had been awakened by the sound of music. He had left his window open, and he went over to see where the music was coming from.

Across the street he saw a Christian church that had been shattered by bombs in the night. It was a hollow shell, with only fragments of walls standing. But amid the ruins and heap of stones was the choir, the preacher, and the little Christian congregation, assembled on a Lord's Day morning for worship. They were singing with triumphant spirit, "The church's one foundation is Jesus Christ her Lord;/She is his new creation, By Spirit and the Word:/From heav'n he came and sought her/To be his holy bride,/With his own blood he bought her,/And for her life he died."

Robertson said that he suddenly was swept up by the dramatic, victorious scene of a spirit that had not been crushed even by hell let loose. "Suddenly," he said, "I saw in the world something that was unshatterable—something that had endured through millenia, something that was indestructible—the spirit and life and power of Jesus Christ within his church." Robertson said he then fell to his knees and said, "Oh, God, now I gather strength and courage to live another day. I will go on because I know that there is another power, stronger than hell, on earth—the power of Jesus Christ."

Well did the great Teacher say, "Heaven and earth shall pass away, but my words shall not pass away" (Matt. 24:35). The world passeth away, and the lust thereof: but he that doeth the will of God abideth for ever" (1 John 2:17).

Church Divisions, Absurd

In a New England city, a wealthy man gave a beautiful colonial church edifice as a family memorial. The kitchen was modern to the nth degree. After the dedication, however, a group of women in the church wanted to add to the kitchen equipment a newly invented electric automatic potato parer. It was a clever device by which potatoes were washed, scrubbed clean, then moved along a belt to a series of knives which peeled the potatoes and finally dropped them into a kettle for cooking.

But there was another group of women who strenuously objected to this newfangled gadget because it eliminated their happy custom of going early to the kitchen and paring the potatoes by hand while they exchanged in social fellowship the news and gossip of the church.

The two groups of women quickly hardened into partisan groups, one determined to have the new potato parer and the other equally determined that the church should not have this potato parer. The controversy became so heated that the women carried their quarrel home and lined up their husbands as participants in the quarrel. As a result, the entire church membership was divided into the pro-potato parer party and the anti-potato parer party.

One day the pastor of this church, greatly depressed, came to see me, telling me he was resigning as pastor of the church. I was astonished and said to him, "How does this happen? You have a beautiful new building, free of debt, a most worshipful sanctuary, and a marvelous modern kitchen."

"That kitchen is just the trouble," he said; and he related the story of the quarrel over the potato parer.

"When I get up to preach on Sunday morning, there before me are the two parties bristling with belligerency—the pro-potato parer party and the anti-potato parer party. Utterly absurd as it seems, their minds are concentrated on this quarrel so that I cannot get through to them with any spiritual message. The potato parer is 'all and in all' to them. It has cut my church sharply in two, and I give up because I can no longer preach the gospel and be heard in such an atmosphere."

Many of our affluent churches are concerned with just such absurdities, while they ignore Christ's mission to the world.

Church and Personal Troubles

It was my happy fortune in the early days of my ministry to have a pastorate on the coast of Maine, where my friendships included a group of sea dogs—the old, weatherbeaten ship captains who had acquired their wisdom from sailing the seven seas in all weathers and climates. They had the farseeing eye; the grim, tight lips; and the experience of men who had to master the destructive forces of nature. Most of them were men who had sailed the old square riggers or the four- or five-masted schooners.

As a land lover I had always expected that in a storm you would head to shore as a place of safety; but I found that the philosophy of the old sea captains was drastically opposite. "What," they would say, "head to shore and dash the ship on the rocks and reefs? No, not in a storm—always head to deep water and open sea. There you can ride out the storm."

In the storms of life I often think of this philosophy. Running to the shore is dangerous—head out to the open sea. Make for the deep water—outride the storm. It is no wonder, then, that a great Christian leader once said to me, "When the church is discouraged, it is exactly the time to strike out on a big adventure." In life, when the criticisms come, head out into the deep.

9.
Prayer

The Power of the Habit of Prayer

Adoniram Judson and his wife, Ann, called on William Carey in India in 1812. As they all walked in Carey's beautiful garden (Carey was a botanist), the Judsons told him how his pioneer life as a missionary had inspired them to offer their lives, too, in missionary service.

They also asked Carey about the three attempts to murder him, the government restrictions on his mission work, and the great fire following five deaths in the mission family. The fire was calamitous in the extreme. Mountains of flames swept all his work to destruction—his printing house, type, plates, paper, and nearly all his manuscripts and translations. The building that had cost so much in labor and money was utterly gone. Young Ann Judson ventured to ask the hardy Carey, "But how could you get so much courage and faith to rebuild all this immediately?"

"Oh," he replied, "it was through the grace of God. As to courage, let me show you the path to my strength."

Along a path in his walled garden, with its great variety of blooming flowers and shrubs, Carey led the Judsons to a quiet bower. "Here now you see my sanctuary of prayer and meditations. Without this I could not carry on through all the hindrances and hardships. I come here at five o'clock in the morning to pray aloud, talking to God and listening to him amid these flowers that he created in all their beauty. I leave the garden about six o'clock for my breakfast and to begin my work for the day. After supper I come again for prayer and meditation with my Bible in my hand." So the discipline of habitual prayer supplied the strength for the first foreign missionary of modern times—William Carey—who once said, "Expect great things from God; attempt great things for God."

Prayer Creative

P. T. Forsythe said, "We cannot be true Christians without being original. Nothing gives us personality like prayer. Nothing makes man so original.

To be creative, we must live with the Creator. Prayer places man in direct contact with God, the Creator, the source of originality."

The Power and Working of Prayer

Charles Kingsley, a clergyman who worked hard for social reform, held his prayer life to be his source of strength. He advised, "Pray as if the devil had you by the throat—to Almighty God to help you out of your despair."

Prayer Interwoven in Our History

When our pilgrim fathers left Delfthaven, Holland, on the first stage of their journey to New England, pastor Robinson led them in a prayer for safekeeping on the perilous voyage, as the brave company knelt on the beach in farewell.

When the tiny Mayflower, after her stormy passage, reached the waters of Cape Cod Bay, the pilgrims knelt in prayer as they solemnly agreed to the Mayflower Compact, which has had such a molding influence on our American government.

Benjamin Franklin called upon the Continental Congress to invoke the power of divine guidance. At the Constitutional Convention, where our nation was taking governmental form, he addressed the Philadelphia gathering in 1787 as follows: "I have lived, sir, a long time; and the longer I live the more convincing proofs I see of this truth, that God governs in the affairs of men. And if a sparrow cannot fall to the ground without his notice, it is probable that an empire cannot rise without his aid."

On a wintry day in Valley Forge a Quaker who was passing along the way saw George Washington, on his knees praying in the woods. Abraham Lincoln never concealed the fact that he was often bowed to his knees, imploring divine help, amid crises of the Civil War.

From colonial days to recent years, schools commonly began the day with prayer, until the Supreme Court forbade the practice. Even so, sessions of the Congress are opened with prayer by the chaplain, and prayers in public are said at the inauguration of our presidents. From time to time our presidents have called upon the people of our nation to observe a day of prayer. He who would divorce America totally from prayer would have a most difficult task.

Prayer and Revival

D. L. Moody, the great evangelist, was led by a singular incident to

enter upon a most amazing campaign in Great Britain. Invited by the
pastor, Mr. Lessey, to take his pulpit on a Sunday, Moody found the
atmosphere frosty and dead. But at the evening service there was a startling
change in the congregation, for the atmosphere was charged with the
lively Spirit of God.

When Moody gave his invitation, people stood all over the church.
He had never seen such an overwhelming response. Concluding that the
people had misunderstood him, to clarify his meaning, Moody asked that
only those who wanted to make a definite decision for Christ meet him
in the inquiry room. People overcrowded the room. Many stood outside.
Then he asked all who were seriously bent on becoming Christians to
return the next night. So many came that Moody preached for ten days,
and over four hundred actually joined the church.

Moody knew that only prayer could explain such phenomenon. Inves-
tigation revealed two devout praying sisters in the church, one of whom
was bedridden. The sick one, instead of bemoaning her misfortune, decided
that she was not helpless; she would devote her life to prayer for revival
in their church. The sisters read of Moody's work in America and prayed
that God would send him from America to their church. And this bold
prayer was answered. When the sick one had asked her sister, "Who
preached at church this morning?" her companion exclaimed, "Mr. Moody
from America. Our prayers have been answered."

Moody's son affirmed that it was this revival that decided the evangelist
to return with Sankey and open his campaigns which had astonishing
and long-lasting results in England, Scotland, and Ireland.

Prayer and Action

In preaching on prayer, Dr. G. Campbell Morgan delighted to tell the
story of the young girl whose brother had set a trap to catch birds in
their garden. Upset by her brother's cruel ways, she let it be known that
she was praying that not a single bird would be caught in the trap. One
morning at breakfast she announced that her prayer had been answered.

"How do you know no bird will ever be caught?" her family asked.
"Because," she rejoined in triumph, "last night I went out and smashed
the trap."

How Many Prayers Have Been Answered?

Yet to be written is an immensely voluminous book collating all the
innumerable answers to prayer. In fact, such a work would run many

times larger than the *Encyclopedia Britannica*.

Two authors of recent times have contributed a beginning to this project: Basil Mathews, a famous writer and Christian layman, and Margaret Lee Runbeck, well-known author of books and magazine articles. Basil Mathews wrote *Prayer Meetings That Made History*, but perhaps Miss Runbeck first gathered answers from a wide range of praying persons.

During World War II Miss Runbeck noticed one morning a newspaper item about some boys who had just been brought in after being taken off a raft from a ship that had been torpedoed. These boys said, "We prayed. That was why a ship went off its course and came over and saw us and picked us up. Whatever you all think, we know what happened when we prayed." This item led Miss Runbeck, a devout Christian, to ponder how many answers to prayer there must be if one could learn of them. Inspired, she initiated a determined search among servicemen and their families the world over. She published the results in a book entitled *The Great Answer*. The circulation was wide, and she found that the book blessed multitudes of people.

Soon she realized that she had touched only the fringe of God's blessing through answered prayer. She lectured widely, and in a *Christian Herald* article she asked about positive answers to prayer. "If you know of such a tangible thing that can be documented, please write to me."

The response was so enormous that she had to get a bigger house and have a bin built especially to hold the letters. After Herculean reading, selection, and hours of confirming interviews, as well as countless visits from strangers who came to tell their stories in person, Miss Runbeck completed a sequel volume, *Answers Without Ceasing*. Work on further volumes ended when God called Miss Runbeck home—her job incomplete, but well done. So the question persists, "How many prayers have been answered?" Tennyson answered, "More than this world dreams of."

Prayer—a Resurrection

Lord, what a change within us one short hour
Spent in thy presence will avail to make!
What heavy burdens from our bosoms take!
What parched grounds refresh, as with a shower!
We kneel and all around us seems to lower;
We rise, and all the distant and the near,
Stands forth in sunny outline, brave and clear;

We kneel how weak! We rise, how full of power.

—Bishop Richard C. Trench

What We Owe to Faith

Living in the New World of the western hemisphere, do we stop to remember that we owe the discovery of this wonderful New World to one man's momentous faith?

Columbus struggled to be heard over a period of eight years, only to be rejected in his dream of a western passage across the Atlantic. First the King of Portugal, then Ferdinand and Isabella and their advisers rejected the proposals. After four rejections Isabella yielded to the pleading of Columbus and offered to surrender her jewels to help his voyage of exploration. He had been ridiculed and treated as a fanatic, and his enterprise had been regarded as a jest. But he kept his faith high and secure. Sailing from Palos, Spain, with three small ships—the *Santa Maria*, the *Pinta*, and the *Nina*—his faith confronted the disbelief of his sailors. Captains and crews of the *Pinta* and *Nina* demanded under threat that he turn back. The sailors and crew of his own flagship, the *Santa Maria*, mutinied against him.

But on October 11, 1492, a night of full moonlight, the lookout on the ship *Nina* shouted, "Tierra! Tierra!"

After eight months Columbus, returning to Spain, was escorted to the royal court of Ferdinand and Isabella at Barcelona. He presented his sovereigns a glorious New World.

O world, thou choosest not the better part:
    It is not wisdom to be only wise
    And on the inward vision close the eyes;
But it is wisdom to believe the heart.
Columbus found a world but had no chart
    Save one that faith deciphered in the skies,
To trust the soul's invincible surmise
Was all his science, and his only art.

Heartfelt Prayer

John Bunyan said, "When thou prayest, rather let thy heart be without words than thy words without heart."

Cleansing Prayer

Prayer will make a man cease from sin; sin will entice a man to cease from prayer.

In the Name of Christ

The name of Jesus Christ is not used as a charm. To pray in the name of Christ means in the Hebrew idiom, "To pray in the spirit, the will, and the purpose of Christ."

Prayer, a Supreme Act

Samuel Taylor Coleridge said, "Prayer is the supreme act and the highest activity of the human mind."

The Shut Door

When Christ urged, "Shut the door, and pray to your Father who is there in the secret place" (Matt. 6:6, NEB), he meant that prayer requires for its deepest value the silence of a retreat, the concentration protected from interruption, and the quietude of the soul's inner sanctuary. What is true of the soul at prayer is also true of the artist and the composer. No one who has seen the original portrait popularly called *Whistler's Mother* will doubt that the artist worshiped his mother. Yet even his mother was excluded from his studio when he was painting. She wrote to a friend, "He is too closely confined to his studio. I am never admitted there, nor anyone else." The shut door is the law of the creative spirit.

Prayer Is a Key to Victory

In *Pilgrim's Progress* Bunyan described Christian as a prisoner of Giant Despair in the gloom of Doubting Castle. Life to Christian seemed hopeless, "Until he bethought him of a key in his bosom, and the key was prayer." As he prayed, deliverance came, as it always does.

Prayer—the Gift Within You

"Who rises from prayer a better man, his prayer is answered."—*George Meredith*

Finish Your Work—a Prayer to Follow Through

Sir Francis Drake's prayer as he sailed into the Harbor of Cadiz was, "Oh, Lord God, when thou givest to thy servants to endeavor any great matter, grant us also to know that it is not the beginning but the continuing of the same, until it is thoroughly finished, which yields the true glories."

Prayer and Work

J. Hudson Taylor, great missionary from China, said: "It is possible to work without praying. It is a bad plan, but it can be done. But you cannot pray without working."

The Power of Prayer

The dying King Arthur speaks to his Knights of the Round Table in Tennyson's poetry:

Pray for my soul!
More things are wrought by prayer
Than this world dreams of . . .
For what are men better than sheep or goats . . .
If, knowing God, they lift not hands of prayer
Both for themselves and those who call them friend?
For so the whole round earth is everyway
Bound by gold chains about the feet of God.

Silence, Solitude, and Meditation

"In the chaotic hubbub of our time," said Carlyle, "souls run to waste." Tennyson's word is pertinent: "Solitude is the homeland of the strong." When Carlyle and Tennyson took long walks together, their conversation was broken by "brilliant" intervals of silence.

Luther translated the words of the psalmist, "My soul is silent unto God," as "Waiting all hushed for God."

Herbert Spencer, the philosopher, had a resolute device for shutting out chatterers. At banquet tables he listened briefly to the person on his right and then to the person on his left. Immediately afterward, from his pockets he produced heavily padded earmuffs, adjusted them over his ears, and solemnly lapsed into meditation. Few have the courage of Spencer, though many have the same desire.

Carlyle said, "Speech is of time, silence of eternity."

"Be silent to the Lord," translated Perowne. "Hold thyself still in the Lord."

Wordsworth invoked "some power to make our noisy years seem moments in the beating of eternal silence."

Paul spent three years in Arabia in meditation and prayer.

Isaac went out at eventide to meditate.

The Impossible Can Be Done

There is a sign in a General Motors plant that reads: "According to the theory of aerodynamics, and as can readily be proven by wind tunnel experiments, the bumblebee is unable to fly. This is because the size of its wings in relation to the size of its body makes flying impossible.

"But the bumblebee, being unacquainted with these scientific truths, goes ahead and flies anyway and gathers a little honey every day."

10.
Death and Immortality

Death, like immortality, might well be considered a reward or a promotion rather than disaster. The decayed fruit has its own glory if the seed is ripe. Death is only tragedy when it precedes maturity.

A Shocking View of Ourselves

Born in Sweden in 1833, Alfred Bernhard Nobel became a chemist and inventor by profession. In 1863 he patented a mixture of gunpowder and nitroglycerin. His big invention came in 1866 when he created dynamite. His renown as the inventor of this terrible power of destruction became worldwide.

Late in his life he received the shock of his life. As he read the morning newspaper he saw on the front page the headline "Alfred Nobel Dead." The subheadline read "Dynamite King dies." The article alluded to him as "the Merchant of Death" and "Inventor of Destruction."

Nobel was appalled as he read a description of the impression he had left by his life of invention. (As it turned out, an over-zealous reporter in France, trying to beat his fellow reporters to the punch, had seized upon news of the death of an Alfred Nobel of the same name and flashed it across the wires.)

The real Alfred Nobel was thoroughly shaken as he studied the account of his life and death. For the first time he realized that he would be remembered only as a man who gave destruction frightening power and who spread death everywhere. Surely, he realized, this was not the aim of a worthy life. He must transform his purpose, and his contribution to the world must be life and not death. So he dedicated his great fortune to peace among nations and founded the annual Nobel Peace Prize. Among the winners of this prize have been the Red Cross, Dag Hammarskjold, Martin Luther King, Henry Kissinger, and Dr. Albert Schweitzer.

If we could all have death giving us shocking views of ourselves, would we not wake up to a transformation of our life's meaning?

Don't Write Hastily

Editors should never write hastily. The following was inserted just before an overcrowded newspaper went to press. "Owing to the overcrowded condition of our columns, a number of births and deaths are unavoidably postponed this week."

Immortality

"All I have seen teaches me to trust the Creator for all I have not seen. Whatever it be which the Great Providence prepares for us, it must be something large and generous; and in the great style of his works. The future must be up to the style of our faculties, of memory, of hope, of imagination."—*Ralph Waldo Emerson*

Meeting the Demands of Death

"And yet here, I think, if a man does really know that God is giving him more and more revelations of himself every day, increasing his faith by all the various treatments of his life, all that is necessary for him is that he should simply accept that constant growth in faith, rejoice each day in the new certainty of God which is being gathered and stored within him, and not look forward, not even ask himself how he will meet the large demands of death and immortality when they shall come. He may be sure that when they come this strength of faith which now is being stored within him will come forth abundantly equal to the need. So a soul need not even think of death if only life is filling it with a profound and certain consciousness of God. The ship in the still river, while its builder is stowing and packing away the strength of oak and iron into her growing sides, knows nothing about the tempests of the mid-Atlantic; but when she comes out there and the tempest smites her, she is ready. So shall we best be ready for eternity and for death, which is the entrance to eternity, not by thinking of either but by letting life fill us with the faith of God."—*Phillips Brooks*

Our Moral Compass

"No," replied President Ford, "I think you are wrong, Billy. We have not lost our moral compass, but we have stopped using it. Now we need to use our moral compass again and head straight for the high destiny it points us to as a nation." It is the neglect of and indifference to our God-given conscience and our rebellion at the moral law of God that lie at the root of our turbulent times.

Lindbergh's Last Adventure

The young man who had adventurous faith in himself and his single-engine plane to cross the Atlantic Ocean in a solo flight also had faith in God. He looked upon his death by cancer as "a new adventure" also.

When Lindbergh knew he had terminal cancer, he went with his wife to his vacation home on one of the small Hawaiian Islands to live out his last days. He engaged a Protestant minister to conduct his last rites, and he himself composed and wrote out the words which the minister read at the burial service. "We commit the body of Charles A. Lindbergh to its final resting place; but his spirit we commit to Almighty God, knowing that death is but a new adventure in existence and remembering how Jesus said upon the cross, 'Father, into thy hands I commend my spirit.'"

Yes, said the great explorer of the air, death is just another "new adventure," which he awaited in eager faith in Jesus. Is not this a true Christian attitude toward death for us all?

Facing Death

Fear death?—to feel the fog in my throat,
    The mist in my eyes?
I was ever a fighter, so—one fight more,
    The best and the last!
I would hate that death bandaged my eyes, and forebore,
    And bade me creep past.
No, let me taste the whole of it, fare like my peers
    The heroes of old,
Bear the brunt, in a minute pay glad life's arrears
    Of pain, darkness, and cold.
For sudden the worst turns the best to the brave,
    First a peace, out of pain,
Then a light, then thy breast.
O thou soul of my soul! I shall clasp thee again,
    And with God be the rest.—*Robert Browning*

Clue to Life Beyond Death

Ada Campbell Rose, onetime editor of the children's well-known magazine *Jack and Jill*, speaking at the Writers Conference in Green Lake, told a story written by Pearl Buck. The scene of the story is in some of the islands of the Pacific Ocean, where volcanos frequently are active and may often be seen belching fire and smoke daily. This fact often presents children with a fear of death. The story is as follows:

"Father, are we not very unfortunate people to live on this island?" Kino asked.

"Why do you think so?" his father asked in reply.

"Because the volcano is behind our house, and the ocean is in front. And when they make the earthquake and the big wave, we are helpless. Often many of us are lost."

"To live in the midst of danger is to know how good life is."

"But if we are lost in the danger?" Kino asked anxiously.

"To live in the presence of death makes us brave and strong," Kino's father replied.

"What is death?"

"Death is the great gateway."

"The gateway—where?" Kino asked again.

"Can you remember when you were born?"

Kino shook his head. "I was too small."

Kino's father laughed. "I remember very well when you were born," he said. "And, oh, how hard you thought it was to be born! You cried, and you screamed."

"Didn't I want to be born?"

"No, you wanted to stay where you were, in the warm, dark house of the unborn. But the time came to be born, and the gate of life opened."

"Did I know it was the gate of life?"

"You did not know anything about it, and so you were afraid," his father replied. "But we were waiting for you, your parents, already loving you and eager to welcome you. And you have been very happy, haven't you?"

"Until the big wave came." Kino shivered. "Now I am afraid again because of the death that the big wave brought."

"You are only afraid because you don't know anything about death." His father smiled. "Someday you will wonder why you were afraid, as today you wonder why you feared to be born."

A Parable of Immortality

Attendants at the Northfield Conference, made famous by Dwight L.

Moody, will recall a notable address delivered in 1927 by Dr. E. Y. Mullins, president of the World Baptist Alliance.

Dr. Mullins described the birth of five little mice inside a grand piano. They were never outside the piano because their life was always within the instrument.

But these mice were somehow touched with scientific curiosity. They began to observe phenomena and to describe what they observed. In this they were good little scientists, because that is what science does—it describes. It tells how things happen; it does not interpret; it does not answer the great question "Why?"

These observant little mice saw a little hammer at one place and a cord in another place. The hammer went over against the cord, and the hammer struck the cord. They saw the cord vibrate and heard sounds emitted by the vibrating cords. Soon another hammer would strike another cord and produce other vibrations and other cords; and this happened over and over.

After these observations they stated the facts: hammer, cords, blows, vibrations, sounds, music; more hammers, more blows on more cords, more vibrations, more sounds, more music. One of the sharpest-eyed of the mice, with a thoughtful expression of a philosopher on his little brow, one day piped the question, "Isn't there something behind all this?"

It threw his four brother mice into consternation. They squealed, "There cannot be anything behind all this because we can see all there is here. It is a closed circle, and we can see how the sounds are produced in this circle of cause and effect." The keen little philosophic mouse was overruled and put in his place.

But one day, his curiosity and his eagerness to find out all truth, no matter where it might lead him, took the little philosophic mouse through an opening inside the piano to the world outside. He looked about, and his eyes nearly popped out of his head. Lo and behold, there was a man sitting on a stool, striking the keyboard with long fingers and causing all the hammers to strike all the cords and thus causing the vibrations to produce music. He scampered back inside and told the other four mice, who remained inside, what he believed he had seen and what he felt sure he now knew. The mice on the inside laughed him to scorn.

"It's absurd; it's ridiculous; it's unscientific; it's impossible. We have observed all the facts and know all the forces, and there is simply nothing personal behind this. This is one great machine and everything works by the laws of mechanics and of physics."

Still the little mouse insisted that he was sure there was something outside the piano which was the first cause and the supreme mind producing all the observed mechanics. His brothers thought he ought to go to an institution for the simpleminded; but since in the mice world no such institutions exist, they decided to tolerate him. They looked upon him as having a second-rate mind possessed of fantastic ideas, which doubtless brought him some queer comfort and satisfaction. But any thoughts otherwise could not be entertained for a single moment by their own tough, superior, scientific intelligence.

Heaven, Release from Earth

Winston Churchill had been through three wars—the Boer War, where he was prisoner, and World Wars I and II. By the time he was eighty-one years old, he felt somewhat weary of the bloody earth. Senator Wiley visited him and told him of the recent discovery of a new planet, said to be nearer our earth than any other planet and only eight hundred light years away. Senator Wiley said to Churchill, "I wonder if this newly discovered planet isn't where heaven is?" The aged, war-weary Churchill replied, "Well, after what I've been through and seen of this earth, I should like to go farther away than that."

The psalmist said, "Oh that I had wings like a dove! for then would I fly away, and be at rest" (Ps. 55:6).

Personal Immortality

Dr. Raymond Calkins of the First Congregational Church, Cambridge, Massachusetts, says of immortality, "Don't you think our loving heavenly Father wants his children with him? Immortality is just as simple as that."

I have had a good many variations to the wedding service suggested to me, but I shall never forget the girl who said to leave out the phrase "till death do us part." I was taken by surprise and asked her whether she did not intend to love the boy until she died.

"Yes," she said, "I do; but I do not intend to stop then." And I left the words out.

Many visitors go to a little cemetery in England where the body of Charles Kingsley, the English churchman and author, lies. His wife sleeps beside him, and there is but one stone over the two graves. On the stone are inscribed these words: "We loved, we love, we will love always."

Charles Reade in *The Cloister and the Hearth* made Claelia cry to Gerard, then Brother Clement, "Adieu forever."

"Forever?" he cried aloud. "Christians live forever and love forever, but they never part forever. They part as do the sun and the earth to meet more brightly in a little while."

W. R. Nichol, longtime editor of the *British Weekly*, wrote to a friend after a great sorrow, "Those who love God never meet for the last time."

> Thou wilt not leave us in the dust.
> Thou madest man; he knows not why.
> He thinks he was not made to die
> And thou hast made him—thou art just.—*Tennyson*

It is not possible to believe that "cosmos should have chaos for its crown."

The Christian believes in personal immortality, not in a vague merging in an impersonal ocean of immortality. Our personal identity shall not be absorbed in a general vagueness of life.

Hell

"There may be a heaven," said Browning. "There must be a hell."

"Hell is God's final surrender to the will of those who are determined to be without him," says Dr. Louis Evans, Jr.

Success Can Be Hell

The story is told of a businessman who was obsessed with greed for money and comfort and who demanded that his every wish be satisfied instantly.

He awoke after death to find himself in a luxurious mansion with servants attending upon his every wish. Money in unlimited quantity was his, and his gourmet appetite was satisfied with every known delicacy. He lounged about on soft cushions without problems, without pains or annoyance, and with no disturbances to his unbroken quiet.

At first he thought that his situation was marvelous, and he liked it. But after awhile he began to be tired of his smooth life and found himself bored beyond endurance by the lack of any duty, obligation, work, pain, problem, challenge, or difficulty.

So he called the owner of the mansion and said, "I can't stand this place another minute. Take me to hell!"

"My dear sir," the owner replied, "where do you think you are now?"

11.
Childhood, Youth, Age

Children

No less a person than our Lord sealed the importance of children for all time. "Let the children come to me; do not try to stop them; for the kingdom of God belongs to such as these. I tell you, whoever does not accept the kingdom of God like a child will never enter it" (Mark 10:14-15, NEB).

Concern for the Child

Christ taught concern for the child. He rebuked the disciples who wanted to create the impression that Jesus was not running a kindergarten. Jesus wanted the children about him, for this is where the Kingdom begins.

There are days when children can be easily hurt. The teacher must always be alert to the child's need.

When Napoleon bombarded Vienna in 1805, the shells he shot into the air over the city struck everywhere. One hit a schoolroom, blasting the walls and windows. An eight-year-old boy by the name of Franz was practicing on the piano in the schoolroom when the cannonball struck. He fell frozen in terror to the floor and hid his face in his arms. While he trembled in terror, there came a reassuring voice calling through the ruined hall. It was the voice of his schoolmaster, saying calmly, "Schubert—Franz Schubert, are you all right, my lad?"

Somehow in these days of hurt and terror to childhood, Christian teachers must be constantly in the spirit of calling through the blasted ruins of our days, "Mary, John, are you all right?" We must remember that children can be hurt and frightened by more things than bombs. The evil ideas abroad in our world, the shows of violence and of murder on television, the screams of death on the radio, the bloodcurdling calls that come into our homes in mob scenes on the screen, and the liquor advertisements can all do great damage to the sensitive child.

Let parents and teachers stand by, safeguarding, inspiring, and reassuring through all disasters with an outstretched hand of love and sympathy: "Mary, John, are you all right?"

Child in Church

Across her, in the solemn hush,
The colors from the windows brush.
Along her shoulders and her head
The spectrums of the saints are spread;
Upon her lap, to her delight
Are shafts of purple, molten-bright.
She studies, on an outstretched palm,
A shimmering and soundless psalm.—*Barbara A. Jones*

Death and Heaven

Dr. Gene C. Bartlett tells an intimate story inspired by life in his own family.

After the death of their grandmother, his older boy was trying to explain to his younger brother the grandmother's death. The younger boy asked his brother, "Well, how did Grandma get to heaven?"

The older boy, still very young, explained it in the following way:

"Well, you see, Grandma put her hands up and up and up and up until she reached just as high as she could go standing on tiptoe. Then God up in heaven saw her reaching up and so he put his hand out toward Grandma and reached down and down and down and down until at last his hand touched hers and then he just put his hand around hers and slowly lifted her up into heaven."

This is a child's explanation of the yearning of the soul to reach God, and of God's yearning to reach down for the soul of man.

Facts About Babies

If he is a *"healthy pink,"* he is also likely to be a *"loud yeller!"*

Theirs Is Willow

It is said that in the modern postwar home, everything will be controlled by an electric switch except the children.

The Best of Both

Youth is not easy. The adolescent is accused of awkwardness, boastfulness, arrogance, and silliness. The fact that youth is also generously blessed is usually overlooked. Actually, youth has the best of both past and future; but, being inexperienced, he seldom knows how to handle that blessing. While still clinging to the innocence and imagination of childhood, he has the developing physique and aspiration of an adult. What our youth most need is encouragement, not criticism.

A Magnificent Generation

This blood-tingling generation of youth—what a magnificent generation to win for Christ!

Superbly capable, they outstrip their elders and their forebears by new and amazing achievements. They possess a potential for Christian service that is terrific. In our exuberant youth the church has a triple-A investment.

Look at them. In stature they are generally taller by two inches than the previous generation. They are more athletic, healthier, and, one must admit, more attractive.

In endurance, they break all records of the past. In my boyhood, it took the best runner 4:12.75 to do the mile race. World-famous Nurmi, in 1923, required 4:10.4 to win the mile. Medics and psychologists affirmed that it would be humanly impossible to do the mile race in four minutes. So, in 1954, a shy youth—Roger Bannister—did the mile in 3:59.4; and shortly after this, another youth cut down Bannister's record. By comparison, what lumbering slowpokes we were fifty years ago!

The ambition to succeed where others fail fires the spirit of modern youth. For a score of years, eleven expeditions tried to scale the height of Mount Everest. In 1924, Mallory, noblest of the brave, perished just short of the topmost summit. Youth took up the challenge, and in May, 1953, staggered to triumph. The tough, enduring feet of Hillary and Tensing stamped on the loftiest peak of the "unconquerable" Everest.

Youth Can Lead the Way to Peace

In one of his public addresses Dr. Basil Mathews told of standing on an ancient bridge under which the Yarmuk River flows to join the Jordan, not far from where John baptized Jesus. The sound of what seemed a shepherd's pipe playing a plaintive air was heard farther up the bank. Looking in that direction, Mathews saw a tall Arab boy strolling along with a flute at his lips. Behind him trotted a small donkey bearing two young girls. After salutations the boy handed Mathews his flute. Strangely enough, it was half a gun barrel.

As he watched his sheep on the hillside, this Arab boy had found a rifle left by some combatant killed on those hills in the Great War. He had filed it in two and then perforated it. Now he was using it to interpret beauty and to give joy to his sisters, to his tribe around the Bedouin campfire; and that day he set it to his lips to entertain foreigners of another race enjoying the hospitality of his land. The instrument of death made by modern mechanical science for the war had become, in the hands of youth, an instrument of peace. An insignificant thing in itself, perhaps. But was it not a modern symbol of the ancient prophecy which, at long last, can be fulfilled on a world scale, that someday: "They shall beat their swords into plowshares, And their spears into pruninghooks" (Isa. 2:4).

Youth in General

George Meredith said, "Keep the young generation in hail." Lord Oxford remarked, "Youth would be the ideal time in life, if it came later." Conrad Aiken called young people "angels who come too seldom."

Sin Specified

The word *sin* has largely disappeared from our vocabulary. Influenced by the new morality, young people cannot comprehend theological definitions of sin. But they do understand that something is wrong with selfishness, jealousy, cruelty, war, hate, and meanness. They can feel their dislike of phoniness, egotism, greed, cheating, lying, stealing, snobbery, disloyalty, race prejudice, and unfairness. They can be led to see that dirty talk, adultery, and abuse of the body by drugs are wrong. Well, let them put the Bible word *sin* against all these vices.

Age, Maturity, and Fruition

Old Age Can Achieve

The prevailing notion that after age sixty-five a person ceases to create and to achieve is soundly refuted by the profoundly impressive record of aged achievers. The roll call of the famous reflects what must be true in some degree of the tens of thousands of lesser-known persons.

Oliver Wendell Holmes, Jr., the most famous judge in his day, served as an associate justice on the United States Supreme Court until he was age ninety-one. He is said to have remarked to a man of sixty-five years, "Oh, to be young again like you."

Winston Churchill became Prime Minister of Great Britain for the second time at age seventy-seven. He visited the United States several times during and after World War II and did not retire until age eighty-one. He died at age ninety-one.

An aged Connecticut woman, affectionately called Grandma Moses, began oil painting at age seventy-five. However, she produced her most famous painting, called *Christmas Eve*, at the remarkable age of one hundred years. She died at 101 years of age.

That mental powers do not always sag with old age is shown in the case of George Santayana, the notable Harvard philosopher who continued to write books up to age eighty-seven. He retired to Spain, his native land, and died at age eighty-nine.

Charles de Gaulle was elected President of France for the second time at age seventy-five.

Frans Hals, the Dutch painter, was thought to be at his peak at age eighty-five.

T. S. Eliot, the modern poet, won the Nobel Prize in literature at age sixty-nine.

Best known among recent American poets, Robert Frost was writing poetry and lecturing up to his eighty-fifth year.

The Italian philosopher Benedetto Croce published two of his works on philosophy at age eighty-five.

Benjamin Disraeli began his second term as Prime Minister of Great Britain at the age of seventy and continued to serve until he was seventy-six, when he crowned Queen Victoria the Empress of India.

Giovanni Bellini painted his greatest works during his last decade of life, when he was seventy-five to eighty-six.

Goya, the famous Spanish painter, continued his profession until he was past eighty. When he was seventy-seven he created some of his most famous masterpieces, although he had to wear double thick glasses and use a magnifying glass.

Clemenceau first became Prime Minister of France at age sixty-five. In World War I France called on him to save the nation and win the war when he was seventy-seven years of age. He visited the United States when he was eighty-one, speaking on the average of ten times a week to enthusiastic audiences.

Verdi composed "Othello" at age seventy-two and "Falstaff" at age seventy-six. Bach did some of his best work in his later years.

William Gladstone, who was four times Prime Minister of Great Britain, served his last term of office when he was eighty-five.

Tintoretto painted his self-portrait when over seventy, while Titian did his self-portrait between the ages of eighty and ninety.

Goethe maintained his physical and literary vitality beyond age eighty.

John Adams became the second President of the United States when he was sixty-two years of age and served until he was sixty-six.

At seventy-nine years of age, Konrad Adenauer was serving as Foreign Minister of West Germany. He retired from distinguished service to his country at age eighty-seven.

Michelangelo reached his peak of talent in his eighties, when he chiseled his famous *Pieta* and built the dome of Saint Peter's. He continued working on his various projects until he was age ninety-five.

The roll call of late, late activists and achievers is almost endless and enormously heartening to all who are contemplating retirement and advancing age.

Old Age—Better Care

An old man, actually 103 years of age, was interviewed just as he was eating a hot dog loaded with mustard and a soft drink. The reporter asked, "If you had a chance to live your life over again, would you have done anything different?" The old man replied, "Well, if I'd known that I was going to live to be 103 I certainly would have taken better care of myself."

Old Age

The well-known *New York Times* correspondent C. L. Sulzberger called by appointment on ex-president Dwight Eisenhower, who had retired to his farm in Gettysburg. Eisenhower was seventy-six years old and was showing visible signs of aging. He greeted Sulzberger in his office on the campus of Gettysburg College. Sulzberger tried to offer a pleasantry about the old general's looking fairly well. Eisenhower actually looked frail and weak. He responded with a smile and said with just a tone of sadness, "Well, you know that a man has three ages. There is youth, then middle age, and then the time when everyone says, 'My, how fine you are looking.'"

Oliver Wendell Holmes wrote a poem about Herman Melville's grandfather. The poem was called "The Last Leaf" and became true of Holmes himself, who lived to eighty-five years of age and outlived his contemporaries—Emerson, Whittier, Longfellow, Hawthorne, Lowell, and others. The last stanza reads:

> And if I should live to be
> The last leaf upon the tree,
>   In the spring,
> Let them smile, as I do now,
> At the old forsaken bough
>   Where I cling.

Mental Growth for the Aged

Discarding the false notion that the aged must live in the past and remain unable to expand in knowledge, Toulouse, France, has successfully established the Third Age College. In the first year the college, oriented to those sixty-five and over, enrolled one thousand students.

The Third Age College is a new division of the University of Toulouse. The aged students (50 percent are over sixty years, and 35 percent are in their seventies and eighties, while a few are in their nineties) say they feel young again doing intellectual gymnastics. The "white hair college" has won respect, and no one pokes fun at it.

One is reminded of the eighty-year-old woman who applied at Princeton Seminary to take Hebrew. "Why at your age," she was asked, "do you want to study this difficult language?"

"Well," she answered, "I expect to go to heaven soon; and I would like to be able to talk to God in his own language."

A Body Not Made with Hands, Eternal in Heaven

When John Quincy Adams, onetime president of the United States, was more than eighty years of age, a friend who called said, "How is John Quincy Adams today?" The ex-president replied, "John Quincy Adams is fine, thank you; but soon he must find a new tenement to live in. This old tenement leaks badly, and the foundations are undermined. But John Quincy Adams is fine, thank you."

Keep Growing

After his retirement Oliver Wendell Holmes had a distinguished visitor.

It was President Franklin D. Roosevelt. Mr. Roosevelt found Mr. Holmes sitting in his study, where he noticed the Chief Justice in his ninetieth year reading *The Allegories of Plato.* The President was amazed and said to Mr. Holmes, "Why, sir, are you reading such heavy diet during your retirement? I would think you would be reading lighter diet in literature in the closing and waning years after a long and demanding career!" Mr. Holmes replied, "Mr. President, I am reading Plato to improve my mind. At the age of ninety I have retired from government and from writing, but I have not retired from growing."

Usable Statistics—Statistically Speaking

There is a story about Madame Perkins' great-grandfather, Edmund Perkins of Maine, who lived to be 104. When he was 99, he ordered a pair of boots made for himself. He gave such detailed directions that the impatient bootmaker exclaimed, "Mr. Perkins, surely you don't expect to live long enough to wear out such boots."

"What's the matter with your statistics? Don't you know that very few men die after 99?"

Resolutions for Old Age!

Not to tell the same story over and over to the same people.

12.
The Family

The Family Basic

You can never have a family of nations until you have nations of families.

The Family Threatened

Dr. Clark Zimmerman, professor at Harvard, wrote: "The extreme we are facing now is the violent breaking up of the whole family system. This is the third such breakup in history. The first was ancient Greece. The second was Rome. If left alone, the family system will break up before the end of this century." The United States has the highest divorce rate of any nation on our planet except Egypt.

Marriage Harmony

A famous marriage counselor is reported to have one crucial question he asks young couples who come to him for premarital instruction. The question he puts to them is, "Who will take out the garbage?"

Family Wealth—Children Axiology

John Fiske of Harvard visited Herbert Spencer, the greatest philosopher of his day in England. Spencer inquired about Mrs. Fiske and the children in America. John Fiske wrote home to his wife, "I showed Spencer the little picture of the picnic wagon with all our children inside. Then I realized how lonely he was without any wife and babies all his own and how solitary he is with all his greatness and I began to pity him. Then as I watched him study that picture and gaze at the children's faces I said, 'That wagonload is worth more than all the philosophy ever concocted from Aristotle to Spencer inclusive.' "

Large Families

A notable preacher said, "I was a tenth child in a family of thirteen. I am so grateful that birth control was not known by my parents, or

I would not be here."

It is pertinent to remember that Washington was one of ten children; John Wesley one of twenty-one children; Shakespeare one of eight; Sir Walter Scott one of eleven; Benjamin Franklin was the tenth child in a family of thirteen; Phillips Brooks was one of nine; Lyman Beecher, father of Harriet Beecher Stowe, was one of thirteen and the most puny baby of them all; Tennyson was one of twelve; and Catherine of Siena one of twenty-two.

The Misjudgment of Others

How often children have been classed as dullards, like Edison, or blockheads, like Wellington, because their elders did not understand them. Think of many children are called dull in school when they only needed glasses or adenoids removed or some proper nourishment. Recall the story of the listless, backward child reprimanded by the teacher, who asked, "What did you have for breakfast?" The child replied, "It wasn't my turn this morning." To know all is to understand all, and to understand all is to forgive all.

Woman

The commentator Matthew Henry with simple eloquence spoke these words on the creation of woman from the rib of man:

"She was not made out of his head to top him, nor out of his feet to be trampled upon by him; but out of his side, to be equal with him; under his arm, to be protected; and near his heart, to be loved."

Husbands and Wives

Marriage Loyalty

Joseph H. Choate, famous diplomat, lawyer, and brilliant raconteur was once asked by a friend: "Mr. Choate, if you were not yourself, who would you rather be?"

After reflecting for a moment he replied, "I would like to be Mrs. Choate's second husband."

God Is Not Dead!

Martin Luther was beset with threats and enemies and was under excommunication. There was a time when his spirits were at a very low point and his mood was utter discouragement. His friends could not seem to shake him out of his despair. Only Catherine, his wife, with a woman's intuition found a way to cure him of his depression.

When Luther came home she did not welcome him. He found his wife in their best room dressed all in black for mourning, weeping as at death.

"What has happened, Kate?" the agitated Luther demanded. "Tell me quick!"

"Oh, the news is too terrible to repeat. I can't bear to tell you," she said.

Shaking her by the shoulders, Luther said, "I demand to know, who is dead?"

"Oh, God is dead," she said, "and I can't bear it, for all his work is overthrown."

"Catherine, this is blasphemy—God is alive!" said Luther, now shocked awake by his wife's attitude.

"Well," she replied, "you have been going around acting as if God is dead, as if God is no longer here to keep us; and so I thought I ought to put on mourning to keep you company in your great loss and bereavement."

"Catherine, our God is alive," shouted Luther again, climbing out of his depression. "Thank you, Kate, for reminding me that the living God is the eternal, unchangeable, Almighty God who faints not, neither is weary."

So many of us today act as if God were dead.

Booth's Wife Shouts "Never!"

When William Booth became a pastor, he refused to stay in a church. He went into the red-light districts of London and preached Christ on the street corners. This brought him much criticism from the clergy, and he was called to appear before his national conference meeting in Liverpool. There his request to be allowed to enter full-time evangelistic work was turned down, and a compromise formula was proposed which would confine him to a small church. The vote was taken and the compromise carried by a large majority. But Catherine Booth, William's wife, rose from her seat in the gallery and waved her handkerchief at her husband. Her clear voice rang out: "Never!" Consternation struck the assembly; but Booth sprang to his feet, waved his hat, and met her at the foot of the stairs. They walked out the door to launch the Salvation Army.

Skeptics asked him, "Where are you going to get your preachers?"

He answered, "Out of the saloons." And he did.

God Is At Your Window

For over two years, thirty depressing months, the wife of Fridtjof Nansen, the great explorer of the Arctic, sat beside her lonely window in Oslo, Norway, endlessly waiting for news from her husband that never came. He had gone north with his ship, but the long-unheard-of party of Arctic explorers was thought to be all dead.

No word came back to Oslo from the silence of the great frozen north. The explorer's wife, Mrs. Nansen, knew that her husband was brave; but she was driven to despair, knowing how cruel the frozen Arctic is. So every morning she went to her window to look out to see if news were coming.

One day there came a little panting, fainting pigeon fluttering down out of the sky. It landed on the window sill. Mrs. Nansen flung the window open. She grasped the shivering pigeon to her breast, holding it close in her trembling hand, kissed its cold feathers, and hugged it again and again. She knew the long, weary miles that the messenger pigeon had flown. After it had been released from the ship, she knew how it had battled its way across the waste of ice and snow, nursing in its tired, little breast a sense of direction for its home destination.

She looked closely at the legs of the pigeon. To its leg was tied a tiny quill. She opened the quill; inside was a bit of tissue paper. On it were written only three words, "All is well."

There are many windows that we can open toward the sky. By birds and flowers, by friends and church, by the Holy Bible, and by Christ himself, God sends his message to us. This is his beautiful message that comes to us from another world: "For God so loved the world, that he gave his only begotten son, that whosoever believeth in him should not perish, but have everlasting life" (John 3:16).

The Family Expanded

Mother's Day

One day I found myself with some hours to wait in the town of Grafton, West Virginia, a railroad center and a coal-mining town. Anyone who knows coal-mining towns knows that these industrial districts have many unpainted houses and not a few sooty and blackened buildings.

Walking along the main street, I spied a church, severely plain in architecture, whose bricks had been blackened with coal dust and age. Suddenly a question flashed upon my mind: What would challenge a minister or give him hope or courage in a dull situation such as this? Then as I drew near the church, I saw an interesting sign in front of the edifice. To my joy and amazement I read that here in this church, the first Mother's Day service in America was held on May 10, 1908.

Miss Anna Jarvis had asked the minister to arrange for a service in honor of her mother. She had been a remarkable woman, a leader in the community, and for many years a Sunday School teacher. The pastor graciously arranged for this special Mother's Day service. The idea was contagious. It was taken up by the Methodist General Conference. Finally, as the idea spread over the land, President Wilson declared a national Mother's Day, which has been observed ever since on the second Sunday in May.

In this little town, somewhat dusty, dark, and dull, a noble Christian woman had caught a great vision. Her vision in this little town has become a national institution. Today it thrills the nation and extends to other nations in the world.

That pastor who encouraged her, and Miss Anna Jarvis herself, demonstrated that God can do wonderful things, even in small towns. He can give all of us, even in lonely places, a chance to make an impact on the world if we are faithful and keep within the circle of his will. All honor to Miss Anna Jarvis, who, in a little town in the West Virginian hills, honored the mothers of the world and has blessed for generations the mothers of men!

My Mother's Soft Face

In James M. Barrie's *Margaret Ogilvie* occurs the unforgettable chapter "How My Mother Got Her Soft Face." This is Barrie's biography of his own mother. He describes the day when the news came that her oldest son had met with an accident. When she arrived at the train to go to him, she was handed a telegram which said, "He is gone."

Barrie's mother returned to her desolate home and submitted herself to the bereavement with a triumphant faith, but she never recovered. She was delicate from that hour. She was strangely ennobled; and her other son, James M. Barrie, writes, "That is how my mother got her soft face—and her pathetic ways, and her large charity! And why other mothers ran to her when they lost a child." She got the faith and inspiration which gave her that soft radiant face from her daily walk with Christ, her Lord and Savior. Her life shines in the beauty of Barrie's description of his wonderful mother, a high soul who climbed the high way. The face can become the index of the character. That is why we love to look at Whistler's famous painting, popularly known as *Whistler's Mother*.

Religious Education or Family Influence

Rev. Martin Niemoller, once a U-boat captain, says: "When I now think on these eventful and decisive years of my life, the question arises whether my call to the pulpit was not inspired through—if not actually decided by—the traditions of my parents' home.

"I am bound to admit that I should scarcely have found my way to it if matters had been otherwise.

"One may have one's own ideas concerning the effect of a Christian upbringing, but my experience has convinced me that a spirit of piety derived from the parental home is a decisive factor in a man's life. Indeed, it is becoming increasingly clear to me how strongly the first recollections of my parents' rectory at Lippstadt impressed themselves on my memory and how their influence on me is increasing with the passing years. Every day began with God's Word, and in the evening it was the last thing we heard."

Doing the Best Things in the Worst Times

Rugby is the great English sport named after the famous English prep school, Rugby. Every English boy at the Rugby School wants to be on the team.

A father who was blind sent his son to Rugby. He attended the games and heard the shouts and roars of the spectators and the cheers for the winning team. He knew his son was a champion player, though he never saw him in action.

Sometime after the son had become the star on the team, the father died suddenly; and the boy was called home for the funeral.

A game was coming up with the rival school of Eton. The Rugby team was in the doldrums, for without their star player they had no chance to win. They could not expect their fellow student to return for the game after such a deep sorrow for the father who had dearly loved him.

But to the team's surprise and joy he returned to the team and played

the game with terrific dedication. "You never played better," said his
teammates. "You played your heart out."

"I had to play my best. It was the first time my father ever saw me
play."

God's Laws: Steadfast—Dependable

Lloyd Douglas once told how he loved to visit a little elderly man
who gave violin lessons. He had a studio, if you could call it that, a small
room set in a long row of rooms where other music teachers taught. "I
liked to drop in on him," Douglas said, "for he had a kind of homey
wisdom that refreshed me. One morning I walked in and by way of greeting
said, 'Well, what's the good news today?' Putting down his violin and
stepping over to a tuning fork suspended from a silk cord, he struck it
a smart blow with a padded mallet and said with conviction, 'That is
the good news today. *That, my friend is A.* It was A all day yesterday,
it will be A all day tomorrow, next week, and thereafter. The soprano
upstairs warbles off key, the tenor next door flats his high ones, and the
piano across the hall is out of tune. Noise all around me—noise—but
that, my friend, is A.' "

Atonement

One day when my son was only three years old, I went to the bathroom
to shave and was horrified by what I saw. There on the washstand was
a puddinglike mess. My young son had taken my tube of green shaving
cream and squeezed it all out onto the marble slab. Then he had taken
a large tube of pink toothpaste and squeezed that on top of the green
shaving cream. Then he had shaken white talcum powder over the mixture.
To make this pudding a bit more fluid, he had sprinkled my ice blue
aftershaving lotion over all and stirred it, leaving a colorful mess all across
the washstand.

This mischief called for correction and punishment; so I called, "Ben,
come here."

Pointing to the mess, I asked, "Did you do that?"

With honesty he said, "Yes."

"You know it was wrong to do this, don't you?"

He answered, "Yes."

"And you know, don't you, that when we do wrong we have to be
punished?"

Without fear he answered, "Yes."

"Hold out your hand, then, and let Daddy slap it," I ordered.

But, to my surprise, he kept his hands firmly behind his back.

Thinking that I should exercise patience, I slowly repeated the routine of the same fine questions, to which he responded with a frank and honest yes. But he still kept his hands behind his back. So I demanded, "Since you agree that you should be punished for being naughty, why won't you hold out your hand to receive the punishment?"

With a logic almost like a lawyer, he said, "Because Mama has already spanked me for doing this."

I put my hand on his shoulder and said, "Young man, you are right. Even the Supreme Court of the United States says no one can be punished twice for the same crime. Go right out and play—you are free."

Christ has already paid the penalty of our sins: "There is therefore now no condemnation to them which are in Christ Jesus" (Rom. 8:1).

Responsibility of Parents

Angelo Patri and most psychologists say that children are taught to tell lies by their parents.

One man remembers visiting his uncle on Sunday. A new neighbor came and asked his aunt if he might borrow the lawnmower. The uncle replied, "Why, if he mows his lawn on the Sabbath, he'll be breaking the Ten Commandments. Go and tell him we have no lawnmower."

Another man remembers visiting his aunt, who reprimanded him for telling a fib. "Do you know," she warned, "what happens to little boys who tell fibs?"

"No. What, Aunty?" he asked.

"Well," she said, "there is a man up in the moon, a little green man with just one eye, who sweeps down in the night and flies away to the moon with little boys who tell lies and makes them pick up sticks all the rest of their lives. Now you won't tell lies any more, will you, for it's awfully, awfully naughty."

13.
Ways of Humanity

Milton's View of Life

On His Blindness

When I consider how my light is spent
    Ere half my days in this dark world and wide,
    And that one Talent which is death to hide
    Lodged with me useless, though my soul more bent
To serve therewith my Maker, and present
    My true account, lest he returning chide,
    "Doth God exact day-labour, light denied?"
I fondly ask. But Patience, to prevent
That murmur, soon replies, "God doth not need
    Either man's work or his own gifts. Who best
    Bear his mild yoke, they serve him best. His state
Is kingly: thousands at his bidding speed,
    And post o'er land and ocean without rest;
    They also serve who only stand and wait."

A General View of Life

The way we face life, our chosen outlook, marks our character and influences our destiny. Two contrasting ways of looking at life are presented in the Bible. Genesis 13:12 says, "Lot . . . pitched his tent toward Sodom"; but in contrast the Bible says that Daniel opened his windows toward Jerusalem (6:10). Lot tipped the scales of his interest toward the fascinations of a wicked Sodom. Daniel turned his gaze toward the holy city through his opened windows. One man had Sodom with all its corruption as his horizon. The other man had the city of God's worship and Temple as his horizon.

The Set of the Sails

One ship drives east, and another west

With the self-same winds that blow;
'Tis the set of the sails
And not the gales,
Which decides the way they go.

Like the winds of the sea are the ways of fate,
As we voyage along through life;
'Tis the will of the soul
That decides its goal,
And not the calm or the strife.—*Anonymous*

Sayings of Great Men

Dean Inge's observation:
"There is not the slightest probability that the big crowd will be found in front of the narrow gate."

If, world weary, we seek a softer spot, we ought to listen to the advice of Phillips Brooks:
"Do not pray for tasks equal to your powers, but pray for powers equal to your tasks."

And no one will fail to get help from visualizing the bent figure of Abraham Lincoln, crushed with the weight of a bleeding nation and with the hate and scorn heaped upon him, as he said,

I do the very best I know how, the very best I can.
And I mean to keep doing so to the end,
And if everything comes out all right in the end,
It won't matter what people say.

Purpose of Life

"The greatest use of life is to spend it for something that outlasts it."—*William James*

"The chief use of this life is to form friendships for the next."—*J. Rendell Harris*

"When we look into the long avenue of the future and see the good there is for each one of us to do, we realize after all what a beautiful thing it is to work, to live, and to be happy."—*Robert Louis Stevenson*

"Some men grow, others swell. The fault, dear Brutus, is not in our stars, but in ourselves, that we are underlings."—*Shakespeare*

"Nothing great was ever achieved without enthusiasm."—*Emerson*

"It concentrates a man's mind tremendously," said Dr. Johnson, "if he knows he is going to be hanged in a week."

A Plan for Each Life

Horace Bushnell, great New England thinker and preacher, said, "God has a definite plan set for every man, one that being accepted and followed, will conduct him to the best and noblest end possible. You exist for a purpose high enough to give meaning to life and to support a genuine inspiration."

Life Need Not Be Dull

Horace Bushnell also said, "Life is always dull and insipid to those who have no great works on their hands to do and no lofty ideals to elevate their spirits."

A big cause makes a man big, for a man takes on the size and the measure of the goals and the responsibilities that possess him.

Let the Fire Come

The fires of trouble, sickness, and adversity are usually thought to be circumstances to be avoided at all cost. But if our lives are hidden in the hand of God, should we fear such fire or welcome it?

An unusual evergreen is the lodgepole pine that is seen in great numbers in Yellowstone Park. The cones of this pine may hang on the tree for years and years, and even when they fall they do not open. These cones can only be opened when they come in contact with intense heat. But God has a reason for planning them this way. When a forest fire rages throughout parks and forests all the trees are destroyed. At the same time, however, the heat of the fire opens the cones of the lodgepole pine; and these pines are often the first tree to grow in an area that has been destroyed by fire.

God's wonderful way of protecting and continuing his creation is often too great for us to understand. But always from the seed new life is waiting for the right conditions. When they come, it is ready to grow and be beautiful again.

Our lives contain many seeds that only God can recognize and that only his wisdom can put to use.

Invest in Lives

A Chinese proverb says, "If you plant a grain, you plant for one year. If you plant a tree, you plant for ten years. If you plant a man, you plant for one hundred years."

Comments on Life

It's not as important to count the apples on the tree as to count the number of trees in the apples.

An unknown person wrote, "Life is hard yard by yard and mile by mile, but inch by inch it's a cinch."

"Life in time remains without meaning," says the Russian scholar Berdyaew, "if it does not receive its meaning from eternity."

Emerson said, "The secret of life is to set the hours against the centuries."

The onetime principal of King's College, London, Sir Ernest Baker, said of his life, "My life has been shaped for me by a guidance which came to me from outside . . . so I must give thanks . . . ."

Things That Count

'Tis the human touch in this world that counts,
  The touch of your hand and mine,
Which means far more to the fainting heart
  Than shelter and bread and wine.
For shelter is gone when the night is o'er,
  And bread lasts only a day,
But the touch of the hand and the sound of the voice
  Sing on in the soul alway.—*Spencer M. Free*

Providence and the Stages of Life

Madame de Sevigne in 1687 wrote most sensitively about the kindly ways of providence.

"Providence," she wrote, "leads us so kindly through all the different stages of our life that we hardly feel them at all. The slope runs gently down; it is imperceptible—the hand on the dial whose movement we do not see.

"If at the age of twenty we were given the position of the eldest member of our family, and if we were taken to a mirror and shown the face that we should have or do have at sixty, comparing it with that at twenty, we should be utterly taken aback and it would frighten us. But it is day by day that we go forward; today we are as we were yesterday and tomorrow we shall be like ourselves today. So we go on without being aware of it, and this is one of the miracles of that Providence which I also love."

Man and Sin

William James, the Harvard psychologist, said, "Biologically considered, man is the most formidable of all the beasts of prey and indeed the only one that preys systematically upon its own species."

14.
Character and Human Experience

A Noble Dedication to One Student

The War Between the States left the South prostrate. Among the institutions which the war had closed down was the Southern Baptist Seminary in Greeneville, South Carolina. In 1865 there were two young professors of vision and daring who went to look over the abandoned seminary building. Standing on the steps just after the war ended, they agreed that with soldiers returning home and peace reestablished, they could reopen the seminary in spite of handicaps. They knew, too, that the enrollment would be small. "But we must have faith and reopen the school," said President James Boyce.

The young professor, John Albert Broadus, responded with anticipation, "Yes, I have been preparing a course of lectures on preaching, for a class in homiletics."

"My dear Broadus," questioned President Boyce, "do you realize that you will have only one student in your homiletics class and that most unfortunately, he is blind?"

"I am sorry to learn that he is blind, but I shall give him my best, just as if there were one hundred in the class," answered Broadus. Day after day he delivered each lecture faithfully to this one blind student. Afterward these lectures were printed and became so popular that it required fifty editions to satisfy the demand for *The Preparation and Delivery of Sermons* by John A. Broadus. This compassionate scholar and servant of Christ became one of the greatest preachers and leaders the South ever produced. The public never forgot his noble dedication to even one blind student.

Character: The Shape of the Person

Character Essential

John Milton wrote, "He who would write heroic poems must make his whole life a heroic poem." Cicero said, "Only a good man can be

a great orator. We either add or subtract the man from what he says."
Thomas Hardy said, "Persons with any weight of character carry, like
planets, their atmosphere along with them in their orbits." Thomas Carlyle
said, "It is not what I have or what I do, it is what I am that is my
kingdom." Your life depends upon your faith, and your faith will depend
upon your life.

Built to Stand

Paul affirmed in 1 Corinthians 3:13, "The fire shall try every man's
work of what sort it is." He stated, "If any man's work abide which he
hath built thereupon, he shall receive a reward."

To build well is to build for eternity.

George W. Boschke was the famous engineer who built the gigantic
seawall to protect Galveston, Texas, from the horrible floods which have
brought disaster to the city. He built this seawall with a sure confidence
of a thoroughgoing engineer and a master workman. From Galveston he
went to Oregon to build railroads in an undeveloped section of the state.
Boschke was in a camp forty miles away from the nearest railroad when
an exhausted messenger rode in and handed a telegram to his assistant.
The message said that the Galveston seawall had been washed away by
a second furious hurricane. The assistant was in consternation and dreaded
to hand the telegram to his chief.

Boschke read the telegram, smiled, handed it back, and said, "This
telegram is a black lie. I built that wall to stand." He turned away and
went about his work. It turned out that the message was based on a false
report. True, there had been a hurricane as severe as that which had
flooded the city before; but Boschke's seawall had not been moved. It
stood firm. "I built that wall to stand," said Boschke and went smiling
about his work amid rumors of disaster.

Every man built upon Christ and every institution built upon Christ
and his truth will stand, come wind, come weather. We have nothing
to fear, for the church is the pillar and ground of truth built upon Christ,
the firm foundation.

Preservation of Freedom Our Responsibility

The story is told of an eight-year-old girl who visited New York City
for the first time. In taking the trip down New York Harbor, she was
most impressed and fascinated by the Statue of Liberty with her lighted

torch, which was given to the United States by France in 1886.

Her home was a patriotic one, and, back home, she could not throw off the deep impression of the Statue of Liberty and her burning lamp held high against the sky. She said to her parents, "Her arm must get awfully tired holding up that lamp all alone. How can we help her, Daddy, way out there, to hold up her hand and keep the light burning?"

The child's question is a penetrating one directed to us all. Unless we are all concerned to uphold our liberties and to keep the light of freedom burning brightly, we shall slip into the shadows and darkness of the light gone out.

The Power of a Single Idea

James C. Hefley in *Christianity Today* recorded an astounding, imaginative achievement by a native of India who became a Christian through a Welsh lay missionary laboring among a tribe of headhunters called the Hmars. Young Rochunga Pudaite, a convert resulting from this missionary effort, graduated from the American Baptist High School in Jorhat and went on to study in St. Paul's College in Calcutta. With this education, the young Pudaite began the translation of the Bible into the language of his own tribe, the Hmars. Winning the attention of Billy Graham and Bob Pierce, he was provided with a scholarship for graduate studies at Wheaton College in the United States.

Here a new vision fired his imagination. Knowing that educated and professional people afford telephones and read English in countries like India, Pudaite began mailing copies of *The Living Bible, Paraphrased,* to persons listed in the telephone books of such countries as India, Nepal, Sikkim, Bhutan, Bangladesh, Singapore, and Malaysia. By May 1974 he had mailed over 1,000,000 copies of the New Testament to these countries. He is now extending his mailings to include Ceylon, Burma, Pakistan, Korea, and Indonesia. In 1975 he planned to complete 2,000,000 mailings of the Bible. With *The Living Bible* being translated into seventy-two languages, he plans to extend his mailings to 200,000 million persons in Asia by 1984. It is the work of one man, with one idea, fired by one great vision.

Yet when he came to America to study, Hefley reported that one missionary who knew he was from the headhunting tribe of the Hmars wrote, "Who in the world squandered the Lord's money to bring a little native like you to Wheaton?" He says he was accustomed to shooting arrows at targets and notes, "We're sitting at the switchboard of the world with direct lines to over 3,000,000 homes."

Hardships Need Not Stifle Creative Blessings

Wolfgang Mozart, master musician and composer, kept alive his indomitable will to create sublime music in spite of the fact that his talents were often snubbed, unappreciated, poorly rewarded, and beset by a haunting host of hardships.

His debts piled up unpaid. In his depression he would beg friends to come to his financial assistance. His wife and child were sick, and Mozart himself was often ill. Begging, he wrote, "I am in a situation I would not wish for my most wicked enemy . . . And if you, my best friends, forsake me, I am lost with my poor sick wife and child."

Yet in the midst of his severe afflictions, his music gushed forth in shining beauty and power. While the high fever racked his body, he continued to compose his "Requiem Mass" up to the day of his death. Yet his friends shamefully neglected the master who had composed fifty symphonies, who played the harpsichord before Queen Maria Theresa when he was only six years old and composed a great symphony when he was only fifteen years of age. Forsaken by friends, he died alone and without money. He was buried in a pauper's grave, not even marked with his name. Yet debts, poverty, persistent ill health, and incredible neglect by patrons and friends did not stop Mozart from pouring forth into the world streams of sublime and fascinating music that still bless the whole world.

Saints

Who is a saint? "A saint," said Leslie Weatherhead, "is one who makes it easier for us to be good."

Schleiermacher put it more pointedly: "Saints are those in whom Christ comes to life and stature."

Adoration

That to which we kneel fills us with its qualities.

"Mankind Was My Business"

Something about the Holy Christmas season warms and stirs our hearts with a new compassion for humanity. "Business," cried the ghost to Scrooge in Dickens' *A Christmas Carol.* "Mankind was my business. The common welfare was my business; charity, mercy, forbearance, and benevolence were all my business."

Profanity

Profanity is a weak substitute for thought and a confession of a limited vocabulary.

Description of Character

Good character is not born; it is shaped by circumstance, much as a sculpture is chipped from marble or pounded and pressed in clay. It comes neither easily nor cheaply. There is in all greatness an element of suffering that is inescapable.

Go Deeper, But It Costs

A friend had a well drilled on his land where he was building his home. A professional well-digger with his latest machinery was engaged to take the job; the agreement was that payment would be gaged by depth, so much pay per foot. He was tempted to save cost by not letting the drilling go deeper than was absolutely necessary. Fortunately, at a depth of 125 feet the digger uncovered a fair supply of tasteful water. There was now a reasonably good flow of water available. It seemed enough for ordinary needs. But then my friend remembered the times of drought when many neighbors' wells ran dry and water had to be hauled from two miles away. A hot, dry summer without rain could happen any year. It had happened before.

He became so disturbed by the thought of possible crisis that he put a question to the professional well-digger. "Sir, I assume that at this 125-foot depth with its fair flow of water, I do not need to worry about normal times. But tell me, in a long season of drought when the heavens give no rain for weeks upon weeks, when the earth burns and vegetation dries up and one by one wells go dry, will this well of mine still give forth this sufficient flow of water for my family needs? Will it supply our needs in such a terrible emergency? For we cannot live a single day without water."

The well-driller said, "No, to take care of your family needs in a terrible crisis you will have to go deeper. You will need to go down where you tap the deeper hidden streams, the lower fountains, and reservoirs of water if you want to be sure that you will not go dry." And then he added,

"But it is going to cost you a lot more." My friend said that that day he learned the important lesson that one must be willing to pay the price to go deeper if he wants those divine resources that will not fail him in the hour of crisis.

The Sheer Edge of Experience

"The solution of any human problem creates another, often greater, problem."—*Ed Mowerer's Law*

"A hard life sharpens the vision."—*Alexander Solzhenitsyn*

> Give me a stout heart to bear my own burdens,
> Give me a willing heart to bear the burdens of others,
> Give me a believing heart to cast all my burdens upon God.
> —*John Baillie*

The men who move the world are the men who do not let the world move them.

The Fruit of the Spirit

Love

True love cannot exist outside the context of friendship and forgiveness.

Great Thoughts for Meditation

"Someday, after mastering the winds, the waves, the tides, and gravity, we shall harness for God the energies of love and then, for the second time in history, man will discover fire."—*Teilhard de Chardin*

"No man is more different from another than he is from himself at different times."—*Pascal*

"To multiply harbors does not reduce the sea."—*Emily Dickinson*

> *Love—Sun*
>
> The night has a thousand eyes;
> The day but one,
> And the light of the whole day dies
> With the setting of the sun.
> The mind has a thousand eyes;
> The heart but one,
> And the light of a whole life dies
> When love is done.—*Anonymous*

Charity to Odd Folk—Infirmities

Be kind to all dumb animals
And give the birds a crumb;
Be kind to human beings too
For some of *them* are dumb.—*Anonymous*

Friendship

In Egypt, at Oxyrhynchus, papyri were uncovered from the sands of Egypt containing sayings of Jesus not recorded in the New Testament. One of these pieces of papyri contained the following sentence which is undoubtedly authentic, "And Jesus said, 'Make a friend.'"

Definitions of "friendship" may be given as follows: A friend is one who knows all about you and loves you just the same. A friend is a person in whose presence you can think aloud.

Proverbs says, "A friend loveth at all times and is a brother born for adversity." Goethe says, "A friend is one in whose presence you say things and your friend says them back better than you said them."

Sir Philip Sidney was the flower of English chivalry and courtesy. There was an English nobleman who wished to have written on his tombstone, "He was Sir Philip Sidney's friend." He knew of no finer distinction than that.

When Paul was a prisoner in Rome, Onesiphorus searched him out and visited him in his prison cell. Paul paid tribute to him in this sentence: "He oft refreshed me and was not ashamed of my chains" (2 Tim. 1:16).

Genial Charles Lamb has expressed the difficulty of disliking people if we really come to know them. The story of Lamb and his friend is pleasant. Lamb, who stuttered when he spoke, was criticizing rather severely a certain person. "Why, Charles," protested his friend, "I didn't even know that you knew him." "Oh, I d-don't. I-I c-c-couldn't d-d-dislike a m-m-man I-I know."

The Failure of Selfishness   *good*

Maltbie D. Babcock said, "Our business in life is not to get ahead of other people but to get ahead of ourselves, to break our own record, to outstrip yesterdays by todays and to do our work with more force and a finer finish than ever—this is the true idea—to get ahead of ourselves." E. A. Wiggam advises, "You will make more friends in a week by getting yourself interested in people than you can in a year by trying to get people interested in you." Dr. H. C. Moule says that the new grammar of the Christian is first person, he (God); second person, you (others); third person, I (self last). George Meredith in *The Egoist* says of Willoughby Patterne, "She beheld him in his good qualities, and his good were drenched in his first person singular. Self is the only prison that can ever bind the soul; love is the only angel who can bid the gates unroll; and when he comes to call thee, arise and follow fast. His way may lie through darkness but it leads to light at last."

Restraint in Speech

The person who insists that he must always say just what he thinks is likely at last to get just what he deserves.

Narcissus

One of the stories that the Greeks liked to tell was the story of Narcissus, son of a river god and of a nymph, distinguished above all others for his beautiful form and face. It was prophesied that Narcissus would have a long, long life if he never looked upon his own features. But this was too much of a temptation for him because he loved himself so much.

One day Narcissus stood a long time and looked at the image of himself in the mirror made by the water. Immediately he fell in love with his own reflection. So he missed the length and fullness of life because he had a narrowly focused attention upon himself as the number one person of importance.

Now whenever we hear of people who fall in love with themselves, who become narrow and selfish, we think of the myth of Narcissus and feel sorry for them because we know they are missing the full joy of life.

Selfishness—Small Potatoes—Too Often Used

One suffocates with spiritual claustrophobia in the narrow presence of those who are drenched in selfishness. You know the type!

I gave a little party this afternoon at three—
'Twas very small
Three guests in all
Just I, Myself, and Me
Myself ate up the sandwiches

While I drank the tea,
And it was I
Who ate the pie
And passed the cake to Me.—*Anonymous*

Forgiveness

John was getting better as he lay in his bed in the hospital. In the bed next to him was another boy named Bill. They had been in the same room for several weeks, and after a time they began to quarrel. Bill said mean things to John, and John said mean things to Bill.

One night when the nurse was fixing John up for the night and tucking him into bed, he was so angry he said to her, "That old Bill is a meanie. I'll never forgive him as long as I live."

The nurse said, "Now, John, it is not right to feel that way. Supposing you should die in the night, then you would be sorry that you had never forgiven Bill."

John thought seriously for a few minutes, and then he said, "Well, all right, if I die in the night, I will forgive him; but if I don't die, in the morning Bill better watch out."

Forgiveness must be very deep and real, not just something we will do if we die.

Deal Gently with the Erring

Deal gently with the erring,
Ye know not of the power
With which the dark temptation came,
In some unguarded hour.
　　Thou hast often sinned and
　　Sinful still must be.
Deal gently with the erring
As God has dealt with thee.—*Anonymous*

Joy

Joy is the overflowing cup. It is the well from which praise arises and the fountain that praise inevitably fills.

Praise for Laughter

Charles H. Spurgeon, famous London preacher, was entertaining a famous New York preacher, Dr. Theodore L. Cuyler. They traversed woodland paths and then broke out into sunlit, flower-bedecked meadows, walking jauntily like two boys out of school. They roamed in carefree high spirits, cracking jokes and exchanging remembered humorous situations in their ministries. Their laughter was rollicking, often breaking into prolonged belly laughs. After one uproariously funny story that sent them both into stitches, Spurgeon suddenly stopped and exclaimed, "Cuyler, let's kneel down right here and praise God for laughter." There among the meadow daisies by the edge of the wood, the two great men knelt down and thanked our God for the precious gift of laughter. Do we remember to praise God for this gift of relaxing power, a joy to the heart, an elixir to the spirit, a release to the tensions, a medicine to the body, and a blessing to the soul? Animals can't understand a joke; and, therefore, they can't laugh. God has reserved this gift for his children.

Giving Praise

"I shall possess my kingdom from afar, giving praise for things withheld."—*Thomas Wolfe*

The Need to Be Praised

"Our praises are our wages," said Shakespeare. Dr. George W. Crane suggests starting a "Compliment Club" with the giving of sincere praise to persons and then making note of the reactions.

A couple about to separate went to a psychiatrist for counsel. The wife complained that the brilliant husband constantly called her "stupid." Said the psychiatrist to the husband, "Hereafter, you eliminate the word 'stupid' and start saying instead, 'You're smart.'" It worked. The couple happily reunited.

Family compliments are necessary. Compliments make our day and perk us up.

Among Benjamin Franklin's wise sayings is this one: "As we must give an account for every idle word, so we must account for every idle silence."

Criticism

Someone advises sandwich criticism between two slices of compliments. It makes it easier to eat.

"Do not be afraid of being too happy," said Charles Kingsley, "or think that you honor God by wearing a sour face."

The power that rolls the stars along speaks all the promises.

Peace

Deep peace of the running wave to you
Deep peace of the flowing air to you
Deep peace of the quiet earth to you
Deep peace of the shining stars to you
Deep peace of the Son of Peace to you.—*Fiona McLeod*

Riches Require Barbed Fences

Paul Getty, the richest man in the world, was worth more than four billion dollars. How did he live?

In a Tudor manor, twenty-three miles from London, Getty lived behind double barbed-wire high fences, patrolled day and night by plainclothesmen and twenty-five German shepherd dogs trained to attack.

"Money doesn't necessarily have any connection with happiness," he observed. From behind his double fences and barbed wire, pack of dogs, and private police force Getty added, "Maybe with unhappiness." His prisonlike confinement suggests he might have been right.

Patience

Patience is made as evident by its absence as by its presence. Anger is always a breakdown on the road of life; patience is the repair truck of which it has need.

Patience and Optimism

In his New Jersey laboratory, deaf Thomas A. Edison made fifty thousand unsuccessful experiments before he produced the incandescent electric light bulb.

A laboratory assistant, impatient and utterly discouraged, complained, "Mr. Edison, we have made now a total of fifty thousand experiments; and we have had no results whatever."

"What do you mean 'no results'"? replied the patient inventor. "We have had marvelous results. We now know fifty thousand things which won't work."

Anger

"Temperament," someone has said, "is 90 percent temper and 10 percent ment." Thomas Hardy wrote in *The Return of the Native*, "Sometimes more bitterness is sown in five minutes than can be gotten rid of in a whole lifetime."

It is a psychological fact that in fifteen minutes of anger one can use up as much energy as in an entire day of zestful work. Anger can disorder nerves, deposit a poison in the blood, and undermine health.

Dr. Alexis Carrell states, "Envy, fear, and hate, when the sentiments are habitual, are capable of starting organic changes and genuine diseases."

Converted drunkard and noted temperance lecturer John B. Gough used to tell about the English lady who spoke to him with the subdued mew of a pet cat but spoke to her servants like an untamed tiger.

A little girl asked, "Mother, how is it when you are cross you say you are nervous; and when I am nervous you say I am cross?"

Anger controlled and constructively used may mean power. "I never write better," wrote Martin Luther, "than when I am inspired by anger. When I am angry I can write, pray, and preach well; for then my whole temperament is quickened, my understanding challenged, and all mundane temptations and vexations depart."

George MacDonald wrote, "There are times when I do well to be angry; but I have mistaken the time." Flabby sentimentalists mourn the wrongs of our times but are not angry enough to do anything about them. John Brown has been called "God's angry man" because he was angry enough at the iniquitous slave system to do something about it. There is not only the love of God; there is also the "wrath of the Lamb."

Goodness

Goodness Not Enough

Someone has said that the world does not suffer so much from the bad ways of bad people as it does from the good people who have very bad ways of being good.

Good Deeds

For some men there is no danger of the left hand knowing what the right hand is doing because the right hand never does anything.

Courtesy

Courtesy is one of those multiple-knit fabrics that true character wears with naturalness and elegance. It depends heavily upon the threads of longsuffering, gentleness, and goodness for its choice texture.

A Test Case of Courtesy

What is courtesy, one may ask? It is not a matter of mere rules, but is a fundamental attitude of being. It is an unselfish spirit that suggests instinctively the appropriate act which conduces to the ease and happiness of others. In the deepest sense it springs from a heart transformed by Christ.

To clarify the meaning of courtesy one may recall F. B. Meyer's story of the young soldier, just promoted from the ranks in India, who was given a farewell dinner by the colonel and officers of the regiment. It was the first time in his life that this common soldier, just elevated in rank, had ever attended a social function in polite society. As the guest of the evening he was tense and shy. He was seated at the right of the presiding colonel, and all dishes were served him first.

The soup having been served, a servant came to the side of the new officer with a bowl filled with lumps of ice. He had no idea for what use the ice cubes were intended and so hesitated. But finally, in answer to the challenge of the servant, "Ice, sir?" he took in desperation a lump of ice and, not knowing what to do with it, put it plump into the middle of his soup. A smile passed around the table. When the bowl was offered next to the colonel, without moving a muscle of the face, he also dropped a piece of ice into his soup. The other guests, taking their cue from the colonel, also dropped ice into their soup. Consequently the new officer was relieved and reassured, now believing that he had made no mistake. This sensitivity to the feelings of others made the colonel a true gentleman. This was courtesy.

Hold Your Tongue

F. B. Smith, a famous Christian layman and well-known speaker, was addressing a banquet of five hundred men in a New England church. He was annoyed by a man who kept running all over the place, greeting newcomers like a self-appointed reception committee. He went about waving his hands in gesticulation. There was a gallery in the hall where women were seated; and this man kept running up and down the stairs to them, too. Smith was so disturbed by this man's acting the way he did that he determined to crack down on him in public rebuke. He had a cutting rebuke on the tip of his tongue several times, but something restrained him.

Finally, when the service was over, people gathered around Smith to thank him for his address. The president of the large men's organization said to Smith, "There is one man here whom I want you to meet. Our large attendance tonight is due to this one man—to his untiring persistence. He has been running all over the city for days selling tickets to this banquet. In fact, for a month he has been busy selling tickets. Unfortunately he is deaf and dumb; but you know, everyone loves the man. He is popular."

Smith thanked God he had held his tongue. If he had let go at the man, he would have had a hostile audience reaction. It would have been a colossal blunder.

Politeness

Someone has said that politeness is listening pleasantly to a man talking who doesn't know what he is talking about.

Will Rogers said, "Everyone is ignorant, only they are ignorant on different subjects."

Courtesy—a Lost Virtue

President Hibben of Princeton invited Buchman of the Oxford Movement to dinner. Buchman, an eccentric believer in divine guidance, came late and unexpectedly brought three other men with him who had not been invited. When he shook hands with Mrs. Hibben, he said, "The Lord just told me to bring these three other men to dinner, too."

Mrs. Hibben, who had not expected the three added guests, replied, "Oh, I don't think the Lord had anything to do with it."

"Why not?" retorted Buchman.

Mrs. Hibben replied, "Because God is a gentleman."

Faith

Faith is inseparable from hope. They are the twins that know what the senses can never demonstrate.

Faith, the Soul's Invincible Surmise

O world, thou choosest not the better part!
    It is not wisdom to be only wise
    And on the inward vision close the eyes;

But it is wisdom to believe the heart.
Columbus found a world but had no chart
    Save one that faith deciphered in the skies.
    To trust the soul's invincible surmise
Was all his science, and his only art!—*George Santayana*

Courage in the Modern World's Darkest Days

Days immediately after Dunkirk were dark days for the modern world. In supreme disaster, all seemed irrevocably lost; and the invasion of England loomed as imminent. England lay prostrate. Forty-seven warships had been sunk in the operations off Norway after Dunkirk. When the evacuation was completed, half the British destroyers were in the shipyards for repairs, while the Royal Air Force had lost 40 percent of its bomber strength. Britain was on the brink of famine, and her armies were without arms or equipment. They had left fifty thousand vehicles in France.

One thing the British did not leave in France was the British character of dogged determination. The British knew how to fight amid overwhelming disasters with lonely but heroic courage.

Churchill spoke for the defenseless islanders: "We shall defend our island whatever the cost may be; we shall fight on the beaches; we shall fight in the fields; we shall fight in the streets; and we shall fight in the hills. We shall never surrender; and if this island were subjugated and starving, our empire beyond the seas would carry on the struggle until in God's good time the New World with all its power and might steps forth to the rescue and liberation of the old."

Afterward Churchill admitted that at that hour England had little more than her soul of courage. "There would have been a shambles in this country because we had hardly a weapon. We had not at that time fifty tanks."

"We shall fight on," shouted Churchill, in that darkest hour.

"With what?" asked the French.

"I don't know," answered Churchill, "but we shall fight on."

Plausible But Dangerous

Somewhere in Spain, it is said, was a castle built on the edge of a three-hundred-foot cliff. This castle could only be reached by a basket let down from the top. Visitors were strapped into a large wicker basket and pulled to the top by a pulley through which ran an old ragged rope.

A visitor, reaching the top and seeing the worn condition of the rope, asked in anxiety, "How often do you install a new rope?"

The casual answer of the attendant was, "Whenever the old rope breaks, of course."

King George V's New Year's Card

King George V during World War I sent out to his friends a New Year's card which had on it the drawing of an open gate. Beneath the drawing was this message:

"And I said to the man who stood at the gate of the year: 'Give me a light, that I may tread safely into the unknown.'

"The man at the gate replied, 'Go out into the darkness and put your hand into the hand of God. That will be better for you than a light and safer for you than seeing the way.' "

Faith in Practice

"I believe in Christianity as I believe in the sun—not only because I see it but because by it I see everything else."—*C. S. Lewis*

"He asks too much for whom God is not sufficient."—*Unknown Saint*

"If there is no God, everything is permitted."—*Dostoevski*

"It is the duty of the human understanding to understand that there are things which it cannot understand."—*Kierkegaard*

"If Christianity goes, the whole of our culture goes."—*T. S. Eliot*

"We go to sleep with the peach in our hand and wake with the stone, but the stone is the pledge of summers to come."—*Emily Dickinson*

Great Expectations

"The realms of the mind are not confined within man's skull."—*Pascal*

"The most beautiful experience we can have is the mysterious. Whoever does not know it and can no longer marvel is as good as dead."—*Einstein*

"The true nature of anything is what it becomes at its highest."—*Aristotle*

Meekness

Meekness is the synonym of humility, the antithesis of conceit.

Humility of True Knowledge

Sir Isaac Newton was one of the great scientists of all time. Most men of science today agree that his great book *Principia* is the greatest scientific book ever written.

Yet of his achievements Newton wrote, "I do not know what I may appear to the world; but to myself I seem to have been only like a boy, playing on the seashore, and diverting myself in now and then finding a smoother pebble or a prettier shell than the ordinary, while the great ocean of truth lay all undiscovered before me."

Perfection—Paradox

The further a man knows himself to be from perfection, the nearer he is to it.

Simplicity

One way to get a reputation is to use big words to make a simple matter hard to understand and to make everything as clear as mud.

Don't Be Self-Righteous

When you get to heaven
    You will likely view
Many folk whose presence
    Will be a shock to you.
But keep very quiet;
    And don't you stare;
Because there'll be most of the folks
    Mighty surprised to see you there too!—*Anonymous*

Desires Ad Infinitum

We want what we want when we want it, but we don't know what we want. The satisfaction of human desire is not the end of desire but the beginning of new desire.

Self-knowledge—Pleased to Meet You

Not every man who knows himself is to be felicitated on the acquaintance.

Related Virtues

All that is admirable in mankind is related to the fruit of the Spirit. All that is commendable presupposes eternal help or challenge.

Youth Hymn Written in Japan

Howard Arnold Walter and his friend Burgess (now Dr. Burgess of Temple University), both fresh out of Princeton, spent their first year in teaching at Waseta University, Japan. They set out on a walking tour of Japan. Japan is a walker's paradise in cherry blossom time. North of Tokyo they stopped overnight at a lovely inn, a Japanese teahouse. Those who know Japan know that most hotels provide geisha girls for the entertainment of guests, and indeed temptations were thrown in the pathway of traveling youth.

That night young Walter thought of the beautiful Christian girl in New York, the daughter of a Methodist bishop, to whom he was engaged to be married. His thoughts went across the sea to his mother, who he knew prayed for him every night. Triumphant over temptation, he sat down and wrote:

> I would be true, for there are those who trust me;
> I would be pure, for there are those who care;
> I would be strong, for there is much to suffer;
> I would be brave, for there is much to dare.

When his year of teaching ended in Japan, the splendid Christian youth came back to America and married his sweetheart, the bishop's daughter. He dedicated himself for foreign missions and chose to work among the mystic Mohammedans of India, perhaps the hardest group to reach. He wore himself down by his arduous labors and died, much too early in life, of heart trouble.

His hymn was the expression of his life. He was true to the Lord because the Lord trusted him. He was brave, for he chose the hardest battlefront.

Wisdom

"The art of being wise," said William James, the famous Harvard psychologist-philosopher, "is the art of knowing what to overlook."

The Vastness of Our Ignorance

The great inventor Thomas Edison said, "We don't know the millionth part of 1 percent about anything. We don't know what water is. We don't know what light is. We don't know what gravitation is. We don't know what enables us to keep on our feet when we stand up.

"We don't know what electricity is . . . We have a lot of hypotheses about these things, but that is all. But we do not let our ignorance about all these things deprive us of their use."

I Will Guide Thee

In the fall of 1951, the World Series was televised across the country—as clearly seen in California as in New York.

In southern California the famous veteran of baseball, Ty Cobb, was watching every movement of the World Series games with the keenest interest. When DiMaggio went up to bat, Ty Cobb perceived that he needed a coaching tip or two. DiMaggio was making no hits.

From a distance of three thousand miles he got DiMaggio on the telephone. Ty Cobb told him how to change and improve his stance and how better to put his eye on the ball at the right moment.

DiMaggio went up to bat twice after that. Taking Ty Cobb's counsel, he knocked the two home runs that won the World Series for his team.

If a baseball expert can observe the small details of the game and help a friend across the stretch of thousands of miles get out of his trap of failure and become a winner, then is it too hard to believe that God is to be trusted when he says, "I will guide thee with mine eye" (Ps. 32:8)?

The wisdom of God and the perfection of his counsels are available to every child of God, to make us victorious.

Fear Not

The remark of David Starr Jordan that "the world turns aside to let any man pass who knows where he is going" may be bracketed with the famous words of Oliver Wendell Holmes: "When a resolute young fellow steps up to the great bully, the world, and takes him boldly by the beard, he is often surprised to find it comes off in his hand, and that it was only tied on to scare away timid adventurers."

An Epic of Christian Heroism and Good Cheer

Wherever Christian gentlemen admire bravery and loyalty today, the story of Sir Robert Scott and his South Pole expedition will be told. Though it ended in tragedy, it left a thrill of glory. Scott and two of his companions, Wilson and Bowers, were finally found asleep in death on the frozen wastes of the Antarctic. Under Scott's shoulder were found three notebooks containing his diaries.

The party had journeyed on foot seven hundred miles back by land to the Pole. They had returned to their sixtieth depot and died only eleven miles from another depot. One of the entries begins, "The cold is intense—forty degrees below at midday. Blizzard as bad as ever. Must be near end—I do not think we can hope for any better things now. We shall stick it on to the end. We are getting weaker, of course; and the end cannot be far. I do not think I can write more. For God's sake, look after our families."

Other diaries were found in the tent, and in one was a letter by Scott to Wilson's wife after Wilson lay frozen in death. "I should like you to know how splendid he was at the end—everlastingly cheerful and ready to sacrifice."

Another entry was a letter to Sir James Barrie, "We are pegging out in a very comfortless spot. Hoping this letter may be found and sent to you, I write a word of farewell. We are in a desperate state, being frozen, etc. No fuel and a long way from food, but it would do your heart good in our tent to hear our songs and the cheery conversation. We are very near the end but have not and will not lose our good cheer. We could have come through had we neglected the sick. The great God has called me."

Fear

An air pilot in the United States Navy was involved in much enemy action during World War II. Again and again he risked his life with unusual courage in aerial combat. Nor did he fear to motorcycle across the continent at high speed to visit his home on furlough. But one winter, when invited by a friend to go skiing, he said with a shudder, "You wouldn't catch me on skis. They're too dangerous. A fellow could get hurt on them!"

A fearless pilot afraid of skiing! It seems strange, and yet not so strange. Actually, he was afraid of the unknown, as are most people. It is to all who face this basic fear that Jesus says, "Be of good cheer, it is I, be not afraid" (Matt. 14:27).

Profiting from Mistakes

To recognize one's mistakes is no real accomplishment. It is, however, a mark of character when one admits them, and a step toward greatness when he can transform them into future good.

No Double Error

"I have made mistakes, but I have never made the error of claiming that I never made one."—*James G. Bennett*

Knowing Our Mistakes

A farmer took his horse out to pasture, but he couldn't find anything to tie the rope to while she grazed. So the farmer tied the rope around his waist while he hoed the corn patch. Pretty soon an auto went by and blew its horn. The horse took fright, kicked up its heels, and started running across the field. The poor farmer was bobbing and bumping along, leaping ten steps in one over the rough field. Finally the horse brought up against the fence of the next farm, where another farmer was hoeing his corn. He looked over the fence at the bruised farmer lying on the ground and said, "Didn't you know any better than to tie yourself to that horse?" Between breaths the man replied, "You know, I hadn't taken three jumps before I saw my mistake."

Excuses for Quarrels

One day I heard about two boys who had been in a fight. When a grown man came along he said, "See here, boys, what are you fighting for, and what is the dispute all about?" There had been the sound of crying and the noise of a slap on the boy's face.

Finally one of the boys said, trying to excuse himself, "Well, I knew that he was going to hit me; so I hit him back first."

Everyone Makes Mistakes

In the famous Rose Bowl football game of 1929 at Pasadena, California, the two teams pitted against each other were Georgia Tech and Southern California. The captain of the Southern California football team was a young man named Roy Riegles. In the course of that game he made a long distance run down the gridiron for a touchdown. He made the only score in the game by this furious dash. But he did not score for his own team; he had run in the wrong direction. You see, in the excitement of the game he had become confused as to which was his own goal. By running in the wrong direction, he actually had made a touchdown for the opposing Georgia Tech team and helped them to win. Deep down inside himself, Roy Riegles knew he had let his team down by making

132 ILLUSTRATIONS FOR PREACHING

this awful mistake.

In the time between the two halves of the game, when the players walk off the field, they always go into the field house, where the coach talks to them. Sometimes he talks to them about their mistakes, sometimes about the plays he wants them to use in the second half of the game.

All the people who were watching the football game in the stadium that day could not help but wonder what Coach Price was saying to Captain Riegles about the terrible mistake he had made. They did not know until afterward that the coach had never even mentioned Riegles' wrong-direction run. Those who had watched the game were at first surprised and then tremendously delighted when they saw the team walking out on the field again. They noticed that the coach had his arm around the shoulders of Captain Riegles. Then they saw the coach give him a pat of encouragement as he went back into the game to play his part the best he knew how.

His Daily Fun

When a distinguished foreigner paid his only visit to America in 1950, a committee of prominent Chicagoans lined up at the railway station to offer official greetings.

As the big man—six feet, four inches tall, and big also in the esteem of the world—stepped off the train, the committee members surrounded him with a gushing welcome. The illustrious scholar, musician, and human-itarian responded with animation, his broad shoulders, heavy shock of hair, and sprawling mustache marking his personality with a unique indi-viduality.

But the committee noticed that his eyes were not wholly fixed on them. Those penetrating eyes were wandering beyond the encircling committee. Something on the station platform caught his eye amid the crowd of travelers.

With politeness but firmness the great man said to the committee, "Excusez-mois" and literally dashed past the receptionists. Diving into the crowd, he stopped beside an elderly woman who was staggering under her load of heavy suitcases and extra bundles. With his big, sensitive hands he grabbed the old woman's suitcases and bundles and, beckoning her to follow him, he threaded a way through the throngs. He led the woman to the coach she wanted to take, lifted up her suitcases into the overhead rack, and, bowing in a courtly manner, wished her "Bon voyage."

Then he rushed back to the astounded committee with apologies for keeping them waiting. "I was just having my daily fun," he smiled. If there were any stuffed shirts in the official welcoming committee, the starch in them was made limp by the perfectly natural kindness of this famous philosopher, physician, and missionary.

This is the way Dr. Albert L. Schweitzer arrived in America!

15.
Nature and the Mind of Man

The World Around Us

God's Mysteries

Instead of debating the existence of God, it may be stimulating to contemplate just a few incredible facts.

There are ten thousand species of birds in the world.

The tiny heart of the wee hummingbird beats a thousand times a minute.

Of the present world population of three and one-half billion persons, no two are identical. The individual thumbprint of each human being is unmatched by any other anywhere. Persons are examples of the infinite variety in nature.

We are tourists on planet earth, which travels in its orbit around the sun at 67,000 miles per hour for a total of 588,000,000 miles in its immense elliptical orbit.

The diameter of our sun is a mere 860,000 miles, contrasted with the blazing sun Betelgeuse, whose diameter is 350,000,000 miles. Our earth's diameter of 7,926.68 miles seems insignificant. Is this all mere chance?

Be Yourself

It is interesting that the mockingbird is often named as one of America's finest singers. He can perfectly imitate even an imported nightingale—thought by many, the poets included, to be the sweetest of all singers; but he degrades his talents by also repeating the rasp of gate hinges and the clack of the typewriter. Though we may quote the phrases of heroes and angels, if we do not find voices for ourselves, we are merely imitators of better men.

There would be no hundred-odd-piece symphony orchestras if every player was limited to the range and values of his neighbors. So it is with Christians. We all have our own ranges and melodies. If we play what others play, our sound is not only unnecessary; it has removed the harmony that we should have contributed from the total song of life.

Precariousness of Man on Earth

Human life is dependent upon the inches of topsoil on the crust of the earth. In many areas this soil is rapidly washing away, and in others it is being exhausted. It takes four hundred years to build one inch of rich topsoil.

Mountains—Challenge, Not Defeat

Several years ago I heard a famed mountain climber explain the fascination that led him to attempt the scaling of major peaks on this and other continents. Seated in a beautiful natural amphitheater near Jenny Lake in Wyoming, my family and I listened to the lapping of waves on sand, let our eyes travel upward toward the forbidding granite summits of the Grand Tetons, and pondered his words.

"You never really understand a mountain until you step on it." He might have added, "until you feel it beneath the hobnails of your boots, until you brush your pack against its battlements; until you grapple with its rarefied air, until you gasp before the ethereal beauty of cloud flags flying from its summit."

At such times one comes to have a feeling for the "still heart of things." He opens his heart to wonder, and he desires to hold it fast and, above all else, never to harden his heart or his senses toward the manifestations of creative might.

Lying on a Judean hillside, the psalmist let the infinite take hold of him. Yielding himself to the mystery of God, he invited the majestic awesomeness of his world to sweep into and over him. There he wrote the sweet lyrics of the psalms. There he came to know, as did Beethoven, that "whatever is to reach the heart must come from above."

Natural Selection or the Plan of God?

The black-capped chickadee is a bird that habitually travels in groups except during the nesting season. Each group of chickadees is known as a tribe and has control over a given territory. Each tribe has a leader and a definite social structure.

When nesting time arrives, the tribe divides; and the birds soon have nests in various parts of the tribe's territory. These little birds mate for life. In stumps of trees often hollowed by the chickadees themselves are the nests, about eight inches deep. The brown-spotted, white eggs are tiny—hardly larger than a bean—and will hatch in about thirteen days.

The young are ready to attempt flying about sixteen days after hatching. Soon the numbers of young dwindle as natural disasters overcome them. Cats, snakes, owls, and hawks account for larger reductions in their numbers. Probably the weaker ones are those lost during this growing-up period. Such is God's plan for keeping birds strong and healthy for many generations.

Another of God's amazing plans is demonstrated in the young. The very rim of their overlarge mouths is colored a brilliant yellow. As long as they must depend upon their parents for food, the yellow is there. This color helps the parents know just where to drop the food they have brought, in one of those rapid dashes from sunlight into the dim cavity of the nest. As soon as the young are able to feed themselves, the yellow vanishes. Only a loving Father could care for his world so well and so thoroughly. Such a Father is God.

Life Everlasting

Most persons have heard of the incredible life span of the giant redwoods and sequoias stretching over 3,000 years. Not so many people know of the amazing longevity of the bristlecone pines of California. Ten thousand feet up on the side of the White Mountains of that state is a tree known as Methuselah because it is 4,600 years old. In fact, it is the oldest living thing known on the planet earth. Before Moses, before Abraham, in the time of the building of the pyramids, this bristlecone tree was living. Each year it still adds a ring to its girth. A genetic scientist was curious to discover whether or not it still has power to reproduce itself. The tree had been struck by shattering lightning and beaten by winter storms. The scientist and his party found that this unbelievable tree had borne a cone. He snapped the cone from the branch and returned home to plant its seeds in his nursery garden. In the spring of 1974 he showed television viewers the twelve bristlecone seedlings grown from Methuselah. After 4,600 years of living, the ancient tree still had vitality to produce children after its own kind.

Like Job, one wonders at the power of long life which God gives to trees. Has he not some plan for those created in his own image that surpasses the life span of a mere tree? Will he give a tree 4,600 years of life and a man only seventy years? "Whosoever liveth and believeth in me shall never die," said Jesus (John 11:26).

The Size of Our Planet

Kenneth F. Wean, assistant editor of the *National Geographic* magazine, suggested that if one were to take a grapefruit to represent the sun and then take a single grain of sand and place it forty feet away from the grapefruit, that piece of sand would be our earth. Or he could take a red cranberry and move it two hundred feet away from the grapefruit; and that would be the planet Jupiter. If he were to take another grain of sand and place it one-third of a mile away, that would be the planet Pluto.

To represent our nearest star, one could take two grapefruits, placing one in Chicago to represent the sun and the other in San Francisco to represent the star.

Respect the Production of Plants

Ecologists estimate that the total annual production of matter by land plants is a dry weight of one hundred billion metric tons. Using the estimate of 5 percent for the plant's mineral content, this means that plants "mine" some five billion metric tons of minerals each year. How does this compare with man's mining endeavors? The worldwide production of iron ore in 1970 was three quarters of a billion metric ton. Even when the 1910 totals for the three nonferrous metals (copper, lead, and zinc) are added to the iron ore tonnage, the worldwide output still comes to less than a billion metric tons. In these terms, then, the plant kingdom is outproducing man by better than five to one.

The Worlds Within Us

The vast brain catalog that we call memory, coupled with the endless, growing tendril known as thought, has given us inventions, science, and modern technology. But the results of man's escalating creativity are destructive as well as constructive. When God, the originator of creation, is left out of man's production, the gift is indeed a mixed blessing.

Man Is Unique

Many animals and small creatures can outmatch man in many capacities. The eyes of the eagle and hawk can see objects far beyond man's vision.

The little grasshopper can jump twenty times his own body's length, while man is fortunate if he can jump twice his body's height.

The remarkable tiny ant can support up to a thousand times its own weight.

Even our dogs have a range of hearing beyond man's; and when it comes to smell and scent, their sense of smell is far keener than ours.

Man may run in a race and make a mile in a little less than four minutes, but a cheetah has been clocked over a similar distance at a rate of seventy-one miles per hour.

The balloon spider can spin a tiny web that will carry him wind-borne a thousand miles.

The common fly can taste with its feet.

But man is unique because God has given him a thirty-billion-cell brain that can think, memorize, invent, receive and store up information, and create technology.

The ant's strength is no match for the man who operates a crane that lifts 3,500 times the operator's weight.

Man's inventive power created the automobile and the airplane that leaves the cheetah's speed a mere nothing.

Man's mind built the microscope and the telescope that dwarf the eye of eagle and hawk.

But man's uniqueness is that he is created in the image of God. Man can communicate in spirit with the God who created him. Man can offer his praise through poetry, music, and prayer—through love, faith, and hope.

The Miracle of Man's Creation

We are too busy to even think about it, but heart specialists tell us that each year our heart pumps 36,800,000 times. In the average age of man as seventy years, the heart beats 2,500,000,000 times. No wonder that Psalm 139 says, "We are fearfully and wonderfully made" (v. 14).

Our brain contains between thirty and fifty billion cells. Authorities differ as to the number of cells. But if we take the lower figure of thirty billion cells, it is enough to make us wonder at our Creator.

The Glory of God in Space

We are all tourists in space, for our rocketship earth on which we are passengers whizzes on its elliptical orbit around our sun at 67,000 miles an hour. Our tour each year covers a neat little journey of 588,000,000 miles. Our planet ship rotates at the same time, giving us the rhythm of day and night so that we travel in comfort on our magnificent journey. We take this journey every year without the trouble of booking with a travel agency; and we arrive at each point with unerring accuracy, unless you count one thousandth of a second in a thousand years an error.

The Immeasurable Greatness of the Creator

Col. James Irwin, the astronaut who walked on the moon, had a transforming experience of the greatness of God when, in his flight, he saw the earth looking only the size of a medicine ball, then no larger than a baseball, and finally the size of a marble. In relation to the universe, he asked himself, "Is this the size of planet earth on which we live—just a marble?"

"When you have had this sight," he declared, "you are overwhelmed by the greatness of God."

Other Flocks?

"Thousands of galaxies exist thousands of light years distant from our earth. There are probably more than one hundred million other planets suitable for higher forms of life."—*Dr. Harlow Shapley*

Space Conquests

Since 1969 the United States has repeatedly had men walking on the moon and talking to earth from the moon.

In 1974 Skylab 3 went on its space mission under command of Col. Gerald Carr. He and his associates spent eighty-four days orbiting space and traveled almost thirty-five million miles at speeds of over twenty thousand miles per hour.

In March of 1974, penetrating further into space, Mariner 10 passed within 450 miles of the planet Mercury, while other spacecraft passed on to the areas of Mars and Venus and sent back thousands of photographs. Yet in the words of Job, we have not yet touched even "outskirts of His garments." Through Mariner 10's photos, astronomers learned more about Mercury in a few hours than mankind had known about it in all the centuries of the past. The pictures were sent back to America through ninety-three million miles.

Gloomy Forecasts

Henry Adams of the family of United States presidents and notable author had remarkable powers of observation and insight. As early as 1862 he wrote to his family, "Man has mounted science and is now run away with . . . Some day science may have the existence of mankind in its power, and the human race commit suicide by blowing up the world "

Half a Mind—the Hydrogen Bomb Is Not the Worst

The Cleveland Conference on World Order, in referring to the hydrogen bomb, declared, "The thing to fear is not the bomb but man." How right this is. It is a fearful thing to fall under the genius of man without God.

Man's Limitations

After the first successful flight to the moon by American astronauts a senator was reported as saying, "We have mastered the universe. Now we can go anywhere we want to." Can we?

Light travels at 186,000 miles per second. "Yet," says Loren Eiseley, "it takes light something like 100,000 years" to travel across our Milky Way. Spaceships many times speedier than ours today could not be manned by astronauts who could live long enough for this immeasureable travel time. But beyond the Milky Way are those intergalactic distances where man could not survive. The interstellar spaces are beyond our dimensions of life and time and survival. However marvelous man's recent advances of knowledge and spaceship travel, we are still imprisoned within unbreakable limitations. Many can only bow before the infinite majesty of the Creator.

God the Infinite Artist or Evolution?

Louis J. Halle, explorer, scientist, and author, in his book *The Sea and the Ice* bases all his observations on evolution. He found no problem with this theory as he studied the birds of Antarctica until he came to the sooty albatross.

Observing this bird, he wrote, "Most references to nature as an artist are mere cant, but there are occasions when one is suddenly struck by the truth of the statement by the fact that it is so in a profound sense. Surely this fantastic bird is the product of something more than the mere utility that is the basis of natural selection.

"What, one may ask, does the work of a Picasso have to do with the work of a blind process like natural selection? The question is pertinent because this bird on the nest is more plausible as the product of the former than of the latter.

"The last and most striking touch of the artist is a small half-ring of pure white against the black head, simply outlining the posterior half of the dark eye. It is the only white on the bird and the only abrupt mark in a design of pastel shadings. The artist, when he reached this point, saw that without it, the bird would appear incomplete as if he had no eye. The eye had to be made to stand out and it was beautifully done (there are philosophical implications here, if we would only apply our minds to them)."

Breath

A Yale instructor was lecturing on oxygen. "Oxygen," he said, "is essential to all animal existence. There could be no life without it. Yet, strange to say, it was discovered only a century ago."

"What did they do then, sir," a student asked, "before it was discovered?"

The Power of Silent Concentration

When remembering outstanding men in the field of science, one thinks of Thomas A. Edison, whose early life as a newsboy was spent in selling papers on a train between Port Huron and Detroit. The conductor allowed the young Edison to fit up a cabinet on the baggage train. Edison stored in his cabinet chemicals with which, in odd moments during the long train ride, he might perform his experiments. One day when the train was making up lost time, it lurched around a curve. The cabinet was loosened from its fastenings and dashed to the floor of the baggage car. A stick of phosphorus fell out and started a fire. When the fire was finally extinguished, the enraged conductor felt that he had had enough. He put young Edison and all his chemical paraphernalia off the train. In his anger he gave the young lad a violent cuffing around the ears. From that day onward Edison dated the beginning of his extreme deafness.

Hard as it was for the young boy to have been made deaf by the rage of the conductor, in later life Edison cherished his deafness. Frequently friends urged Edison to undergo an operation at the hands of a famous specialist, who promised a cure for the scientist's deafness. At last, reluctantly, Edison made the appointment. But when the day came Edison did not appear at the surgeon's hospital. Instead they found him at work in his laboratory. He had decided that the operation should not be performed. One of his greatest assets in his inventions had been the deafness which shut out noise and distractions of the world around him, allowing him to concentrate intensely on his study and experimentation. He would not allow what had become a hallowed silence and a creative deafness to be taken away from him.

The Inventor of the Telephone

When you pick up the telephone to talk with your friends, don't forget that they called the inventor Alexander Graham Bell "Crazy Bell." Well, who was "Crazy Bell"? He was born in Edinburgh, Scotland, the third of three brothers. His two brothers died of tuberculosis.

Young Alexander fell ill, too. The doctors gave him only six months to live. So his father, Professor Bell, took his son to Canada, to the town of Brantford in Ontario, where he recovered his health in the strong, pure air.

When he was twenty-three years of age, Alexander went to live in Boston, where he became acquainted with the philosopher Ralph Waldo Emerson and the poets Oliver Wendell Holmes and Henry Wadsworth Longfellow.

Here Alexander became interested in trying to help those who were deaf to be able to speak and to read lips. One of his students was a beautiful girl named Mabel, who had never been able to hear anything since she was a baby. While young Alexander Graham Bell was teaching his deaf student, he fell in love with her.

Meanwhile, he turned his talents to invention; and out of his interests in voice and in sound he hoped to develop, through means of wires and electricity, the power to transmit the human voice over wires. To many people the idea was so utterly ridiculous that they called him "Crazy Bell." Mabel's father and mother told Alexander that he could not marry their daughter unless he stopped wasting his time trying to make inventions or could perfect his invention before too long.

One night Alexander Graham Bell's keen ears heard the faint sounds of a human voice coming over the wires and mouthpiece he had invented. Soon friends became interested and provided the money for the building of the first telephone. Many people still made fun of it, and Western Union rejected it as just an "electrical toy."

At last Mabel's parents consented to their marriage, and Alexander Graham Bell had the double joy of winning the girl he loved and seeing his invention of the telephone a success.

Alexander Graham Bell never forgot that if he had not been keenly interested in trying to help other people and trying to show deaf people how to read lips and how to talk, which compelled him to study the human voice and the transmission of speech, he might have never invented this marvelous instrument we call the telephone.

Changing the Environment

"Human nature can be changed," asserts Professor Hocking of Harvard, confirming the gospel. Changed lives can also change the environment.

"Ye are the salt of the earth. Ye are the light of the world," said Christ. A striking example of a changed environment through the life of a single individual is portrayed by Edward Bok in his autobiography as he describes the Island of the Nightingales.

In the stormy North Sea off the coast of the Netherlands lay a ledge of rocks where many a vessel had been wrecked. Pirates who looted vessels inhabited the island and murdered crews. Finally the Netherlands government determined to rid the island of pirates and assigned Edward Bok's father, a young Dutch lawyer, to do the job. It was a grim place, barren of trees or of any other living green thing; but the young lawyer cleaned up the island and decided not only to make it his home but to make it beautiful. He led seafaring men to inhabit the island and said to them, "We must have trees." Since they were too busy with their fishing, he was compelled to say, "I'll have the trees if I must plant them myself."

"Your trees will never live," said the islanders. "The north winds and storms will kill them all." But plant trees he did, a hundred the first year. The second year he planted more; and each year for the fifty years he lived on the island, he planted trees. The birds that were so often storm-swept by the turbulent North Sea rested on this island in the course of their flight and found protection here against the tempest. As the trees grew tall through the years, the island became a bird sanctuary. In time, bird lovers from all parts of the world came to this island to study the thousands of birds that rested here.

Then one night a singular thing happened. A pair of storm-driven nightingales found refuge in the island. In gratitude for their refuge, they remained on the island and raised their young nightingales. Within a few years the island became a colony for nightingales. At eventide the women and children would walk out among the trees to listen to the evening notes of the birds of golden song. Throughout Holland and Europe, the fame of the Island of Nightingales spread. Meanwhile Bok led the islanders to build quaintly shaded streets and to convert the sunbaked wastes into verdant lanes of beauty. The American artist William M. Chase brought his pupils here each year. "In all the world today," he asserted, "there is no more beautiful place."

This Bok married and had a family of thirteen children, whom he sent out into the world with a message that they must make every barren place beautiful and every rocky land a refuge for the birds of the air and the song of the nightingale. His grandchildren went to the four corners of the earth and one of them, Edward Bok, built the famous bird sanctuary in Florida.

But it all began when one young Dutchman determined to make a barren reef of rocks a refuge of beauty and a cathedral of golden song.

16.
Illumination from the Arts

Authors in Their Positive Mood

Christ: the Supreme Shepherd

John Ruskin wrote of a beautiful custom that prevailed in his day among the shepherds of the Alpine Mountains and, for all I know, may still be observed in Switzerland. Many shepherds pasture their flocks on the high slopes of the Alps. There is always one shepherd who is highest up on the mountain. He takes his shepherd's horn, places it to his lips, and sounds through it the notes signaling, "Glory to God in the highest." As the melody floats down on the pure evening air, the shepherd on the next lower pasture catches the sound and, placing his horn to his lips, relays the melodious message "Glory to God in the highest" to the next lowest pasture. Up and down the valleys, Ruskin said, for the distance of a hundred miles on a clear evening, there sounds the sweet message "Glory to God in the highest" as the shepherds unite in their evening worship.

We have heard the voice of the supreme Shepherd, the highest and the holiest, the loftiest among men, and the voice of God to our souls, sounding forth the message "Glory to God." So may we catch the blessed word of Christ and pass on its eternal music from soul to soul until our church, our community, and our world shall resound with the glorious praise of God. Then when the chief Shepherd appears, may we receive the crown of glory that shall never fade away.

Unconscious Influence of the Lowly Upon the Mighty

Thomas Carlyle's greatest work was undoubtedly his two volumes on the French Revolution. The work is a masterpiece. Carlyle loaned, in the original manuscript form, the second volume of his French Revolution work to his friend John Stuart Mill to read and to criticize. Mill, in turn, loaned it to another friend to read. This friend thoughtlessly left the precious manuscript on a table where a servant, cleaning the room, threw it into the fireplace. Carlyle was hurled into despair when he learned that all his hard labor had vanished into smoke and ashes. For days he sat in his room in London in incarnate gloom, unwilling to see or talk with anyone. He seemed incapable of any further literary effort. But one day, from his pessimistic slump, he looked across the acres of London roofs. There he saw a mason building a wall with painful patience, laying brick upon brick.

What astonished Carlyle was that in all this slow monotonous work the mason was singing as blithely as a lark. Here was a man happy and persistent in humdrum work which brought no public applause. The man's joyous devotion to his patient, daily toil struck a dagger blow to Carlyle's pessimism. He awoke from his stupor of despair. He got to his feet and went back to his desk, suddenly fired with a new passion. He wrote over again the entire second volume of the French Revolution. It is indeed his masterpiece.

But so far as anyone knows, the painstaking, singing bricklayer never knew what he had done for Carlyle and, through Carlyle, what he had done for the literary and historical world.

Good Communications Vital

A true story has often been told of a famous circus elephant in England named Bozo. He was undoubtedly the largest elephant brought from India to England, and he attracted large crowds. Though he was so huge, he was friendly and gentle with everyone, particularly with the children who fed him peanuts.

Then one day the elephant suddenly changed character, becoming irritable, angry, and dangerous. The children were no longer allowed to feed him, and he almost stamped his keeper to death in the cage. The circus owner finally decided that there was only one answer to this problem, which was to put Bozo to death. Being desperate for money and having a crude outlook on life, the circus owner of Bozo advertised that his execution was to take place and sold tickets to spectators to come and witness the event. The news got into the London papers, and all the tickets were sold out days before the advertised killing.

On that day, with the crowd assembled to watch, three men with long rifles came forward to aim their guns at Bozo's head. Just at that moment a short man with a derby hat and a mustache stepped from the front row, lifted his hand, and said, "Don't shoot that animal; he is not a bad animal; he is a good elephant." Even though the owner insisted that the elephant was too dangerous to live any longer, the little short man with the derby hat and the mustache said, "I still say this is a good elephant, and I will prove it to you by going into his cage alone."

The owner, ready for anything that would give the crowd a sensation, agreed on one condition. "You must write out a paper, absolving me from all responsibility if anything happens to you." A paper was produced, and the short man wrote out the required statement and signed his name.

The short man took off his derby and laid it on the floor. The owner opened the cage door, and the short man went in while the crowd held its breath in suspense. The elephant started to charge while the man opened his mouth wide and shouted strange words that no one could understand. The man kept on repeating the words, and Bozo stopped just before reaching the man. He seemed to be listening to these strange sounds. Then the crowd heard a new sound from the elephant. It sounded like crying, and the elephant shook his huge head from side to side. The crowd said it sounded like the cry of a baby. The short man patted the elephant's long trunk. Then Bozo picked up the little man in his trunk and walked around the cage three times with him.

The short man with the mustache came out of the cage, shut the door, put the derby back on his head, and said to the owner, "I told you Bozo is a good elephant. He is homesick and lonesome. You see, coming from India, he doesn't understand English. I spoke to him in the Hindustani language, which brought back India, his homeland, to him. Now you find a man who can speak Hindustani and bring him here once a month to talk to Bozo in that language, and you will always have a good elephant."

As the man in the derby hurried away from the circus tent, the owner remembered that, in the excitement, he had not noticed the name of the man who signed the paper. He looked at the paper carefully and read the signature: "Rudyard Kipling."

Faith in Times of Trouble

Everyone knows Robert Louis Stevenson as the author of *Treasure Island*. Not many people, however, know that his father was the official engineer who built lighthouses around the coasts of England and Scotland.

On one occasion, as inspector of lighthouses, he took his young son, Robert Louis, with him on his ocean trip. They sailed on the ship *Pharos*. Near Bell Rock, off the Irish Coast, the ship was struck by a September gale which lasted for twenty-seven hours, putting all the passengers in fearful peril. The lad, Robert Louis, was terrified.

Finally the boy's father went up on deck and made his way aft as best he could, somewhat panic-stricken by the furious spectacle of the ruthless waves.

Only one person was on deck, the captain; and he stood aft the foremast to which he had lashed himself with a rope, to keep from being washed overboard. Stevenson's father fought his way around through the howling gale until he could scrutinize the captain's face. Then he slowly fought his way along the deck and back into the cabin below.

"Will the ship break up and sink, Father? And we all drown?" asked the young Stevenson.

"No," said his father, in calm assurance. "we will outride the storm. I looked into the pilot's face, and he smiled."

The Seeing Versus the Blind

Elizabeth Barrett Browning wrote:

> Earth's crammed with heaven,
> And every common bush afire with God;
> But only he who sees takes off his shoes,
> The rest sit around it and pluck blackberries.

"Appointment in Samarra"—as told by George Vendeman

The legend says it happened in the streets of Baghdad.

A merchant sent his servant to the market. But soon he returned, trembling and greatly agitated, and said to his master, "Down in the marketplace I was jostled by a woman in the crowd, and when I turned around I saw it was Death that had jostled me. She looked at me and made a threatening gesture. Master, please lend me your horse; for I must hasten away to avoid her. I will ride to Samarra and there I will hide, and Death will not find me."

The merchant lent him his horse, and the servant galloped away in a cloud of dust.

A little later the merchant himself went to the marketplace and saw Death standing in the crowd. He said to her, "Why did you frighten my servant this morning? Why did you make a threatening gesture?"

"That was not a threatening gesture," said Death. "It was only a start of surprise. I was astonished to see him in Baghdad, for *I have an appointment with him tonight in Samarra!*"

On Being Forced to Work

Charles Kingsley said, "Thank God every morning when you get up that you have something to do which must be done, whether you like it or not. Being forced to work and forced to do your best will breed in you temperance, self-control, diligence, strength of will, content, and a hundred other virtues which the idle never know."

Loneliness

Thomas Wolfe wrote of loneliness, "Naked and alone we came into exile. In her dark womb we did not know our mother's face. From the person of her flesh have we come into the unspeakable and incommunicable prison of this earth. Which of us has known his brother? Which of us has looked into his father's heart? Which of us has not remained forever prison pent? Which of us is not forever a stranger and alone?"

Miracles Everywhere

Walt Whitman, great American poet, wrote:

Why, who makes much of a miracle?
As to me I know of nothing else but miracles . . .
To me every hour of light and dark is a miracle,
Every cubic inch of space is a miracle.

Be Practical

Gilbert Chesterton, the famous English author, was once asked what book he would want to have with him if he were cast adrift on a lonely island in the Pacific and were permitted to have only one book. Knowing that he was a devoutly religious man, someone said, "I suppose you would choose the Bible." He said, "No, not the Bible."

Knowing that he was a literary man, the interviewer then said, "I suppose you would choose a copy of Shakespeare." "No," he said. "Not a copy of Shakespeare." Then, "What would you choose?"

Chesterton replied, "If I were stranded on a lonely island in the Pacific, the book I would want to choose of all the books in the world would be one entitled *A Manual on How to Build a Ship*." Life is full of very practical needs, which must be taken into consideration along with our ideals.

Authors in Doubt

Modern Man's Predicament

Archibald MacLeish, poet, dramatist, and former librarian of the Library of Congress, said, "We have advanced science to the edges of the inexplicable and hoisted our technology to the sun itself. In brief, we are prosperous, lively, successful, inventive, diligent, but nevertheless and notwithstanding, something is wrong; and we know it. We feel that we have lost our way in the woods, that we don't know where we are going, if we are going anywhere."

An Unbeliever's Tribute to Jesus

Renan, the French author (not a believer himself), wrote, "Jesus is in every respect unique, and nothing can be compared with him. Be the unlooked-for phenomena of the future what they may, Jesus will not be surpassed. Noble initiator, repose now in thy glory, thy work is finished, thy divinity is established. A thousand times more living, a thousand times more loved since thy death than during the days of thy course here below. Thou shalt become the cornerstone of humanity insomuch that to tear thy name from this world would be to shake it from its very foundations. No more shall men distinguish between thee and God."

Faith Will Out

Although the poet Shelley signed the word *atheist* after his signature, the death of his friend and fellow poet John Keats left him shaken to his depths. Despite his profession of atheism, he wrote lines which seem to make God the One who "remains."

> The One remains, the many change and pass;
> Heaven's light forever shines, Earth's shadows fly;
> Life, like a dome of many-colored glass,
> Stains the white radiance of Eternity . . .
> That Light whose smile kindles the Universe,
> That beauty in which all things work and move.

Goethe's Prophecy

Goethe, in his conversations with Eckermann, said in 1828, "I see the time coming when God will no longer take any pleasure in mankind and when he will have to wipe out everything once more and make a fresh creation."

Belief Controls Action

The notion that it doesn't matter what a man believes is well punctuated by a remark of Dr. Samuel Johnson to his sidekick Boswell.

Speaking of a man who had just denied the existence of a moral order, Johnson said to Boswell, "If he does really think that there is no distinction between virtue and vice, why sir, when he leaves our house, let us count our spoons."

God Is Not Mocked

GREAT ✓

Sinclair Lewis, the author of *Main Street, Elmer Gantry, Babbitt, Arrowsmith*, and other books on the American scene of the 1920s and 1930s, finally won the Nobel Prize.

As a young, tall, redhaired, cocky author, he became acquainted with Dr. Stidger, a Methodist pastor who was drawing large congregations in his church in Kansas City and who often used rather sensational methods. Dr. Stidger had the idea that he might be able to help Sinclair Lewis in religion, though, as a matter of fact, Sinclair Lewis despised all religions.

One Sunday evening he invited Sinclair Lewis to speak for ten minutes in his pulpit. Sinclair Lewis stood up and, holding his watch in his hand, proclaimed that there is no God. He then said, "I will prove this to you, for I will defy God to strike me dead in the next two minutes." He held his watch open, counted the seconds, and created an awful silence in the church in the face of this blasphemous challenge to Almighty God.

The answer is, of course, that God did not strike Sinclair Lewis dead in the two minutes that Sinclair Lewis demanded. However, in the following years, Sinclair Lewis became a heavy drinker, had several severe breakdowns, and could not live in any one place contentedly. He would buy a home and then move out of it in a restless, roaming way. He could not get along with his own sons, went through divorces, and finally died in Rome with only his secretary present at his deathbed. Not a person, not a friend came to see him while he was in the hospital; not a person attended his body as it was sent to the crematorium to be reduced to ashes. He died in delirium, forsaken and alone after years of slowly dying.

Quotables: Books and Authors

William Lyon Phelps at age eighteen first read Thomas Carlyle. "I became all a-tremble," he wrote, "and I heard the trumpets blow through the thick night."

Curtis Lee Law called books "the card of admission to the selective circle of all who have lived wisely and well."

Criticism May Be Pleasant!

"I would rather be attacked than unnoticed. For the worst thing you can do to an author is to be silent as to his works."—*Samuel Johnson*

Truth Immortal

Oliver W. Holmes said, "Truth gets well if she is run over by a locomotive, while error dies if she scratches her finger."

"Criticism is a study by which men grow important and formidable at very small expense."—*Samuel Johnson*

Quotables

James Russell Lowell said, "A weed is no more than a flower in disguise."

"Never explain," said Robert Louis Stevenson. "Your friends don't need it, and your enemies won't believe you anyway."

To sportswriter Grantland Rice is credited the lines:

> When the one great Scorer comes to write against your name,
> He writes not if you won or lost
> But how you played the game.

"The London Literati appear to be very much like little potatoes," wrote Samuel Taylor Coleridge, "that is, a compost of nullity and dullity."

"Conceit is just as natural a thing to human minds as a center is to a circle."—*Oliver Wendell Holmes*

Mark Twain said of some, "They were good men in the worst sense of the word."

Quotables: with Tongue in Cheek

House of Seven Gables

An old lady from Missouri was being taken by a guide through Hawthorne's House of Seven Gables in Salem, Massachusetts. She whispered to the guide, "Can you tell me if any members of the Gable family are still living?"

Editor

"*Editor:* A person employed on a newspaper whose business it is to separate the wheat from the chaff and to see that the chaff is printed."—*Elbert Hubbard*

News

News is anything that makes a person say, "For heaven's sake!"

Manuscript

Something submitted in haste and returned at leisure.

English Literature—If They Only Knew!

Two students were just going into the classroom for an examination in English literature. "Great Scott," said one, "I've forgotten who wrote *Ivanhoe.*"

"That's easy," replied the other. "I'll tell you if you'll tell me who the dickens wrote *A Tale of Two Cities.*"

Book Titles Confusing

In a Boston bookshop, a devout woman tried to purchase Canon Farrar's book entitled *Seekers After God*. Since no copy was available in the Boston store, the bookseller offered to wire their New York store for a copy. They wired, "Have you any *Seekers After God?*" The answer wired back was, "No *Seekers After God* here; try Philadelphia."

Well-wisher

Swift wrote a friend, "May you live all the days of your life."

Musicians

Builders and Dreamers

We are the music-makers,
    And we are the dreamers of dreams,
Wandering by lone sea-breakers,
    And sitting by desolate streams;
World-losers and world-forsakers,
    On whom the pale moon gleams:
Yet we are the movers and shakers

Of the world forever, it seems.
With wonderful deathless ditties
We build up the world's great cities,
    And out of a fabulous story
    We fashion an empire's glory:
One man with a dream, at pleasure,
    Shall go forth and conquer a crown;
And three with a new song's measure
    Can trample an empire down.—*Arthur William O'Shaughnessy*

God Makes All Things; Even Our Mistakes Work Together for Good

One summer the composer Edvard Greig was staying at a small Norwegian hotel. Also at the hotel was a restless child who annoyed the guests by constantly trying to play on the piano, fumbling discordant, broken renditions of the classics. Criticism of the child was frequent among the guests. One day in particular the child's playing was getting on the nerves of every guest, almost beyond endurance.

Suddenly Greig came into the room, quickly sensed the situation, and, walking softly up behind the child, spread his long arms on either side of her. With his hands he began to play, weaving such beautiful harmonies around her discords that her false notes were lost in the music of the master. The guests were hushed with admiration and fascinated by the sudden transformation of discords into fantastic harmonies. When the child finished, Greig presented her to the audience as the player and called for applause for the child.

So God, our kind heavenly Father, weaves his grace around our fumbling efforts, and round about our insufficiency his sufficiency, and round about our restlessness his rest.

Courage—Inspiration

Handel's *Messiah* is rated by critics "a supreme masterpiece of all music." Yet how few who listen in rapture to the glorious music of the *Messiah* realize the hardships of the famous composer! Handel had to struggle against a sea of troubles. He had to fight rheumatic pain, mental illness, and severe financial loss. Twice his health broke, and twice he was in financial straits. Some time before he composed the *Messiah*, with money all gone, his right side paralyzed, and his creditors threatening to imprison him, he was tempted to give up his work. But then suddenly he was

seized with new courage and a tremendous inspiration. He arose from
his depression to compose his greatest work, *Messiah*. Later, after three
eye operations, he became totally blind; yet he did not give up composing
and directing. He directed *Messiah* for the last time when he was blind.
Eight days later he died in London. His was the conquest of courage
over defeat.

Self-discipline

A violinist of a Boston symphony orchestra reported that its conductor,
Serge Koussevitzky, was very insistent before each concert on taking time
to get every instrument in perfect tune. He has been known to take an
entire hour just to get every instrument in tune before a concert. This
is one reason why the one hundred and fifty instruments of the Boston
Symphony Orchestra sound as one voice.

Koussevitsky refused to eat heartily before a concert. Before a concert
he would eat only a little porridge with honey and butter. He reserved
his meal until after the concert was over. Though he is no longer the
conductor, his techniques remain famous.

Mastery Requires Hard Discipline

Virgil Fox, considered one of the world's great organists, is famous for
his interpretive arrangement for the organ of Bach's "Come Thou Sweet
Death." He was only twenty-seven years old when he was asked to play
at a convention of the American Guild of Organists. He decided to play
Bach's masterpiece with a special arrangement of his own composition.
In this performance his reputation and his future career would be at stake.

In order to interpret Bach with intense feeling and to render with highest
skill the intention of the great composer, he secured use of the world-famous
John Wanamaker organ of Philadelphia. For eight consecutive days, from
early evening until dawn, Fox practiced feverishly until he disciplined
himself to make his rendition as nearly perfect as humanly possible. When
the young organist finished playing before the convention Bach's "Come
Thou Sweet Death," the ovation was overwhelming. His fellow organists
had never heard anything like it. His reputation was established at age
twenty-seven as one of the world's greatest organists. His discipline had
won the mastery.

Our Best for God

It is said that Caruso was once urged to sing for charity for a Veterans'

Benefit for wounded soldiers. In order to move persuasively to induce Caruso to accept the appointment, the committee who waited on the great opera singer made it clear that he need not strain himself as he would for a paid performance.

"You won't need to rehearse—they are only soldiers," they said, "and you can sing anything that is easy. You need not be at concert pitch. But your name will bring the crowd."

Caruso bristled with indignation and lifted his big barrel chest. He exploded, "Caruso always sings his best, and if Caruso comes he will give you his best or nothing."

The temptation to settle for our second best with God is always present. The old hymn was right in its admonition, "Give of Your Best to the Master."

Concert Pitch

Dr. Howard Ruopp of the *Chicago Sun* Evening Club tells a story of a lonely herdsman far up in the solitudes in the state of Montana. When he was not occupied by herding sheep, he was asked what he had to occupy his time. He replied, "Well, I play my fiddle and listen to the radio." Then he related how one day his fiddle got out of tune and he had the problem of getting it back into tune again. This original Montanan hit upon the fantastic idea of writing to the sponsor of a familiar radio program and asking him if it would not be possible to sound A over the radio so that he could tune his fiddle. The sponsor saw the advertising value of complying with such an unusual request and forwarded a letter to the cabin on the Montana range, notifying the herdsman of the day and the hour when he would hear A sounded over the radio for his benefit. There sat the herdsman far away from friends, amid the solitudes, with an ear cocked to the radio. On the waves of the blue thin air he heard at the specified time the sound of A once, then a second time. That was all, but the herdsman turned the screw on his violin and brought it up to concert pitch.

If our souls would but listen and worship, the tune-swept strings of our hearts would respond to the master melody of God; and we would bring our lives up to concert pitch. This is why we need worship and the fellowship of prayer. All the discords of the world slacken the strings and get us out of tune; but when we wait upon God in the silence, "he restoreth our souls."

Painting

An Honest View of Ourselves

When Oliver Cromwell, the Lord Protector of Great Britain, sat to have his portrait painted, he said to Peter Lely, the painter: "I must give you positive instructions to paint me honestly. I desire you to use all your skill to make the portrait truly like me. Do not flatter me at all, but put into the face the pimples, warts, roughness, and everything as you see me."

So the strong face of the painting comes through with warts and all. Most of us pay the photographer to take out the wrinkles and blemishes. We shun an honest picture of ourselves.

The Danger of Deterioration of Character

A dramatic story has often been told of the experience of one of the old master painters—an event often ascribed to da Vinci. In any event, a famous artist spent years painting a large canvas of the Lord's Last Supper. He first painted in the face of Christ as the center of the group around the table. To do this, he searched until he found a young man of transcendent purity, strength, and loveliness to serve as his model. Then he worked through long months and years, painstakingly painting in each of the disciples one by one.

Knowing his greatest difficulty would be the painting of the face of Judas, he postponed this to the last. To find a Judas model he knew he must search among the low and debauching resorts of evil. He must find a face so deprived and traitorous that it would describe Judas without a doubt. He found such a man and engaged him for a sum of money. When the painting was ended and the artist was giving the final payment to this model for Judas, the evil-faced man said, "I remember when you painted me once before when I served as your model."

"Oh, you are surely mistaken. I've never painted you before."

"Oh, yes, you did," he replied. "The time before when you painted me, you painted me into your picture as Christ." The long years of the pursuit of a vicious life of sin had made a terrible change in his face.

Sensitivity Through Suffering

On seeing Millet's famous painting of the *Angelus,* one is moved by the poverty of the peasants in the potato field at the evening curfew bell. Despite their hardships, the peasants are bowing in silent prayer. This masterpiece has touched a million hearts with a response of reverence and compassion. Yet few know that while his brush was bringing irresistible appeal to an immortal canvas, Millet was deep in poverty. He wrote a friend, "We have only enough fuel to last us for two or three days, and we do not know how we are going to get any more." His mother was dying, and he could not borrow enough money for carfare to visit her in her last hour. He became so depressed that he seriously considered suicide. When we look at the *Angelus,* we cannot fathom the pain of emotion each stroke of his brush cost him. Pain is so often the price of triumph.

The Sweet Singer of Georgia

The poet and musician Sidney Lanier, who sang of *The Crystal Christ, The Greatness of God,* and who wrote the unforgettable ballad of Gethsemane *Into the Woods My Master Went,* as a young man was a student at Johns Hopkins University, Baltimore. He was a flutist of extraordinary skill and played in the Symphony Orchestra at Baltimore.

One day as the orchestra was rehearsing and the symphony was building up under the baton of the conductor to the grand crescendo with drums, clappers, cymbals, horns, trumpets, all at full organ, a whimsical thought impishly entered the youthful mind of Lanier. Within himself he said, *What difference does my little flute make with its tiny music in the midst of this thundering roar? Even if I should stop, my playing would never be missed.* Still holding the flute in position at his lips, he ceased to blow or to play his part.

Instantly, quick as a steel trap, the conductor banged his baton angrily, halted the music, pointed directly at Lanier, and said, "Where is the flute?"

Lanier had not counted on the extreme sensitivity of the conductor to the music of the smallest instrument and his instant awareness that it was missing from the grand harmony.

So too our Christian service may seem to us so small and obscure that we are tempted to doubt its vital importance to God. But even if we only play the flute in God's great orchestra of Kingdom service, still we must be certain that the failure to do our part will somehow mar the completeness of his harmonious plan. His omniscience has constant regard for even the little part we are playing in his eternal purpose.

Insight

J. M. William Turner, the famous English painter noted for his lavish use of color, was once painting a sunset. A tourist came by and stopped to observe him at work on his canvas. "I don't see where you get all those many colors," said the stranger. Turner replied coldly, "Don't you wish you could."

Sculpture and Architecture

Perfection the Goal

One stands in Rome before the gigantic white marble statue of Moses by Michelangelo, overwhelmed by its living force of character and qualities of leadership. The marble is not lifeless but alive with power. One marvels at the genius whose chisel wrought this personality out of a block of stone.

But Michelangelo, surveying his work, was far from satisfied with his achievement. In sudden temper he struck the knee of Moses with his chisel, crying, "Why do you not speak?" There is still seen the long narrow dent made by the chisel on Moses' knee. The master sculptor kept an ideal impossible to achieve, and perfection eluded his grasp.

So, too, we may never reach perfection in this life, but Christ has set our goal—"Be ye perfect even as your Father in heaven is perfect" (Matt. 5:48). Since God commands this perfection, he must give us an afterlife in which to achieve this goal. This is one hope of immortality.

The Head of John the Baptist on a Platter

Of the 364 pieces of sculpture wrought in bronze and marble by Auguste Rodin, one of his smallest but most dramatic works is his head of John the Baptist on a platter.

Severed from the neck, the head lies on its side on an elliptical bronze platter, the right-hand brow resting on masses of wavy hair as on a pillow. As the hair flows down, its waving length nearly covers the ugly scar made by the cruel sword.

The skin is tightly drawn in death over the gaunt face, but the sunken eyes are closed in serenity as if in sleep. The horrifying brutality of the beheading of John is forgotten in the nobility of the finely chiseled face. The limpid hair wreathes the face in almost a halo and thus mantles the scars of Herod's swordsman. Suddenly one sees that the lifeless head is awake at the mouth. The mouth is open, and the muscles of the mouth seem to be forming great words. Intuitively I bent down my ear to hear what the prophet was saying. Indeed, the face seems to have been formed around the mouth. This is the striking dramatic achievement of the sculptor—the still-severed head speaks as in loud voice for the world to hear.

The sculptor made vivid what John meant when he said, "I am the voice of one crying" (John 1:23).

So the prophets are never silenced by the swords of the brute monsters or the fatty dictators who think to smother the Word of God. Even in the silence of the museum hall, viewing this bronze head on the platter, I seemed to hear a loud voice crying, "Repent ye . . . prepare ye the way of the Lord" (Matt. 3:2-3).

Perhaps, too, Rodin was reminding us that expedience never becomes the prophet of God. If we speak God's truth today, we may lose our heads tomorrow—maybe not with the sword, but there are other ways of demoting the prophets and beheading them. Right now there are not many John the Baptists on the horizon. Oh, for a voice again crying in the wilderness!

The Hand of God

The sculptor Rodin was especially interested in the study of hands. One of the finest and most famous of these is the magnificent *Hand of God*, in bronze. It shows a great sensitive hand holding a clod of earth from which the entwined forms of a man and a woman are emerging, seeming to pull themselves free from the hampering sod. The hand both holds and shapes them.

There is tremendous contrast between the dreamy, inert, semiconscious state of the created and the clean-cut vigor and vitality of the Creator's hand, which comes up with a thrust out of earth that suggests the life force itself.

Vertical lines predominate in the work, lifting the glance upward. Different textures of skin, hair, and earth create further contrasts, and beautiful green highlights accent the dark bronze.

Standing before this great work I saw not Adam and Eve in God's hand, but the whole race and destiny of man. Hastening to identify myself with them, I felt the security of being there; and I rejoiced in the realization that "he's got the whole world in his hand."

Watch Your Influence—Profanity

Anyone who admires ceramics must have thrilled again and again at the sight of beautiful Wedgewood china—the creations of the famous Wedgewood potteries of Hanley, England. Many pieces of Wedgewood are priceless.

An English lord, on one occasion, came to visit the famous Wedgewood pottery works; and Josiah Wedgewood, the owner of the establishment, assigned a teenager to conduct the nobleman about the plant, explaining to him the various procedures of the unique Wedgewood products. The nobleman was a careless blasphemer, and his remarks at first shocked the lad; but, as the tour of inspection continued, the lad finally recovered from his shock and began to laugh at the foul and profane language of the nobleman.

Josiah Wedgewood had overheard much of this profanity; and when the two returned to the central office, Wedgewood gave vent to his indignation in a dramatic way. He picked up one of the magnificent Wedgewood vases and pretended to offer it to his lordship, but suddenly he let it slip from his hands and smash to a thousand fragments on the floor. When the nobleman who had wanted the vase expressed his anger at the disaster, Wedgewood replied with only slightly concealed indignation, "My lord, that was a most precious vase, and it represented hours of work by my most able craftsmen. But though it is ruined, it can be restored, or I can have another made just as good. I will make you another vase just like this, but let me tell you that you can never give back to this boy who has just left the room the simple faith and pure heart which you have taken away from him by your foul, impure, and blasphemous language, which you poured forth upon his young soul."

Your Identity and Self-confidence

Frank Lloyd Wright, perhaps the best-known architect in his day, was under cross-examination in a case in court in Chicago.

One cross-examiner said, "Give us your name."

"Frank Lloyd Wright," was the answer.

"Your occupation," requested the lawyer.

"The world's greatest architect," was the answer.

"How can you say that?" demanded the lawyer.

"Because I'm testifying under oath," replied Wright.

Actors of Christian Faith

Robert Young, the popular TV Marcus Welby, M.D., had his life remade by his return to God and the counseling of a patient wife.

Figuratively speaking, he believes that God may touch a man on his shoulder in warning to reverse his life-style.

Filled with inner fear and terror, he suffered "psychosomatic headaches—headaches," he said, "that hit the inside of my skull like hammers." He felt that his unbearable suffering led him to a point where he couldn't help changing his life. Very simply he confesses that it was a turning back to God.

On tour as an actor in Chicago, he had, he revealed in an interview, "a complete emotional and mental breakdown." He endured "total physical exhaustion, depletion and lack of energy," and he felt that he had "reached the end of the line." As he expresses it, he had painted himself into a corner. In the hospital, once past the crisis of death, the confidence of his wife gave him new hope.

As he began to get better, he felt that he had shed his old self and was reborn into "a new sort of life, like a brand-new baby."

There are miracle cures, and Robert Young believes they "occur every day." He declares that our young people must be given "a new realization that they are children of God." He rejoices in the Jesus movement. "Turning on to Jesus," he affirms, "can transform an individual."

This crisis of our times threatens to make "our planet a burned-out cinder," he warns; and he feels that it is as if God or Jesus is saying something very important, telling us that we've "gone too far." The answer is "the return back to God."

Don't Underestimate People

A famous actress known for her delicate beauty and dainty voice, Billie Burke, was sailing on an ocean liner to Europe. A man lounging on the deck chair next to her was frequently coughing and obviously had a bad cold. She turned her charm on him and said, "Sir, you really should wrap yourself up in good warm blankets, drink lots of hot lemonade, and then you should get into bed and sweat off that dreadful cold. You know a bad cold can turn into pneumonia. But if you take my advice, you'll get well. I'm Billie Burke."

The man smiled and replied, "I thank you, Miss Burke. I'm Dr. Mayo."

17.
Social Problems

Alcoholism

When the New England band of missionaries landed in the Hawaiian Islands, they came with the Puritan spirit of establishing schools, churches, printing presses, and moral standards. A few of the missionaries, however, saw no scriptural injunction against drinking wine and liquors in moderation. But after observing the moral degradation and debauchery caused by intoxicating liquor among the native population, reaching even to the Hawaiian king, they could no longer remain participants in their personal habits; and they all became total abstainers.

Perhaps something like this happens today among many Christians. They may find liberty to drink in the New Testament, but when they see twenty-five thousand persons slaughtered annually on the highways by drunken drivers; when they see two million women and three million men as alcoholics; when they see the ten-billion-dollar annual liquor business profiting from the home tragedies caused by hard liquor, they prefer to have no part in the evil. To them, to see a tall, broad-shouldered, handsome man with a brilliant mind a slave to drink, useless to society, a magnificent ruin—this to them is an ultimate tragedy, the horrifying work of intoxicants. They simply will have no part of it, even for a moment's selfish pleasure. Their own consciences are best at rest when they abstain totally, though they hold no judgment over Christians who differ with them.

A Mounting Menace

In recent years the annual sales of the liquor industry in the United States have increased from nine billion dollars to nineteen billion dollars. Each year there are fifty-five thousand persons killed by auto accidents. Of these twenty-three thousand are killed by drivers under the influence of liquor. One million persons each year suffer major injuries through auto accidents. Of these one-half, or five hundred thousand, are given major injuries by accidents caused by drunk drivers. In half of all the murders in our nation, drink is an active cause—either because the killer or the victim or both have been drinking.

Further, according to *Time* magazine, many companies are alarmed by the fact that alcoholic employees are costing them "countless billions a year."

Another disturbing fact is that lowering the drinking age has swept thousands of young people into the drinking habit. The upsurge of drinking by those under twenty-one has caused a skyrocketing of arrests for drunken driving in some states. For instance, in Michigan there was an increase of 141 percent in arrests the year following the lowering of the age of drinking. In San Francisco suburbs, high-school freshmen are reported showing up for class "drunk every morning."

Add to this the fact that there are now almost ten million problem drinkers or alcoholics in the United States. Between two and three million are women alcoholics.

A new and difficult challenge faces the church where many members of the congregations are social drinkers, on the way to becoming problem drinkers. Young people are constantly urged to drink by their peers. Kids are lured into drinking pop wines which have 9 percent alcohol flavored with sweet fruit. This alcoholic content is twice that of beer and makes an easy step to hard liquor.

With nineteen billion to play with, the liquor industry spends uncounted millions in massive advertising to infect the public mind. At a press conference at the Capitol of California in Berkeley, Dr. Joel Fort made allegations that the industry buys favors from legislators through lobbyists. He made serious charges, declaring "well-financed lobbyists [of the liquor industry] pay for the campaigns of many legislators, ply them with free booze, food, and women, and tell them how to vote if they want to keep getting favors." Is California the only state where this may be happening? Not likely.

A gigantic parade of the victims of drunken driving over the last ten years would show over two hundred thousand skeletons marching past and five million crippled, blinded, wheelchair victims, and other major injured hobbling past, to say nothing of the alcoholics who destroyed themselves.

Inflation

Remember when a postal card was a penny? A hot dog cost five cents in 1940, and today the price is at least thirty cents. Some persons easily remember when a letter cost two cents to mail and a nickel bought a loaf of bread. As a student I earned ten cents an hour. In 1941 President Roosevelt signed a new minimum wage law—thirty cents per hour. The latest minimum wage is $2.30 an hour. Taxes on houses have increased from $300 to $15,000 in many cases. A man's suit of clothes was purchased in 1935 for $10 which today costs $150. The end is not in sight. Remember when gasoline was 15 cents a gallon? You name what it is now.

Our Endangered World

The Dumping of Waste

In Aberfan, Wales, an enormous pile of shale and the residue from the processing of coal were dumped for decades on the side of a mountain. On October 22, 1966, the four-hundred-foot pile began to slide and gathered momentum until the two million tons of slag crashed into the village, engulfing the school and the miners' homes. One hundred and forty-four persons were killed in this crash of waste.

In New York City about five million tons of garbage and waste are collected each year. The commissioner of sanitation has warned that in seven years all sites for dumping will have been used up.

In the United States we have the burden of disposing of 130 million tons of junk. Dumping into the sea has polluted all oceans, including the Antarctic Ocean.

Ecology and Pollution

One thousand acres of the famous Ponderosa Pines in the mountains of the San Bernadino National Forest died in 1970 from the polluted air or smog blown in from Los Angeles, eighty miles away.

Three hundred thousand miles of transmission lines in the United States occupy four million acres of land. It is estimated that by 1990 two hundred thousand miles of lines will be added, making a total of over seven million acres of land held for transmission lines.

Lake Erie became a dead body of water foully polluted. The expenditure of millions of dollars is slowly working toward a cleanup. The cost of cleaning Lake Michigan, at times almost a cesspool, is estimated at ten billion dollars.

Food and Mineral Resources for Tomorrow

Wilbert McLeod Chapman, oceanography authority, declares that the ocean can supply more animal protein than can a human world population several times larger than what we have now, providing the needs for every man, woman, and child in a daily ration. The problem is one of catching the resources and of equitable distribution. It is not a problem of the productive capacity of the ocean, Chapman affirms.

His claim that the production of food from the sea is increasing "at a much more rapid rate than the human population" will surprise many.

One-half of the world's population suffers from malnutrition, largely due to a deficiency of essential amino acids provided by animal protein. The ocean could produce four times the present catch of fifty-five million tons of edible fish. There are enough fish in the sea, given equitable distribution, to solve the world's malnutrition problem, in the opinion of well-known authorities.

Minerals from the sea, including oil and gas, gross about $4.5 billion annually. Most of these minerals come from the continental shelf. The deeper ocean remains to be explored for added mineral production.

Affluence—Poverty

Riches and Poverty

In 1970 the gross national product of the United States passed the trillion-dollar mark. This makes our nation not only the richest nation in all the earth. It also makes us one-third richer than the next richest nation, Sweden.

Yet in the same year, 1970, Health, Education, and Welfare reported the number of people in the United States on welfare as 8.4 million. The lowest tenth of our population (20,000,000) get 1 percent of the national income, while the highest tenth get 30 percent of the nation's income. Fourteen million Americans live in the ghetto, and economists say that this number will increase to twenty million by 1985.

America's Unequal Affluence

Although the United States has only 6 percent of the world's population living on only 6 percent of the geographical earth, our country possesses

52 percent of the world's material wealth, and we use more than 30 percent of its energy. This affluence concerns many thinking Christians.

The World's Hunger

Sixty out of one hundred people in the world do not have enough to eap. Sixty percent of the world's population have a diet that falls below the 2,200 calorie mark. Of these 30 percent, or one-half, must eat below the 2,000 calorie mark, which is recognized as the slow starvation level. It has almost become trite to say that in Africa, the Near East, and the Far East, millions go to bed hungry, wake up hungry, and slowly starve. "When I really think about this," said a famous English minister, "I cannot enjoy the dinner set before me."

Medically the world is starving for healers. In Africa there is an average of one doctor to 24,000 persons. Life expectancy in India is thirty-two years. In the United States it is now seventy-four years, due in large measure to good and sufficient food and excellent medical care.

D. L. Moody's Poverty and His Mother

Four years after he was born, Dwight L. Moody's father died leaving his widow with nine children, the oldest of whom was thirteen. There were only two acres of mortgaged land surrounding the little hillside home where Moody's mother struggled in poverty to raise and educate her family. Left with a burden of debt, her creditors were unbelievably cruel, taking everything she owned "including the kindling wood from the woodpile." Yet this brave, sturdy woman gave one son as a great evangelist and founder of schools and another as the president of a great college, not to mention the honorable careers of her other children.

Other Problems

The Spiritual Gap

The spiritual "gap" is our greatest gap, and it widens progressively with the decades. Sixty years ago, Sunday movies and Sunday sports were illegal in most states. After the wide-open commercialization of Sunday came the elimination of Bible reading and prayers in our public schools. Christians are now a minority group in our population. The weekly long lines of penitents awaiting confession in the Catholic church are gone. Protestant and Catholic students for the ministry have declined in numbers varying from 25 to 50 percent.

Lower community standards, once abhorrent in America, now permit hard-core pornography, movies that portray the most intimate sex, "gay" groups and homosexual churches, mixed nude bathing, and blasphemies on television. Removing "In God We Trust" from our coins and eliminating chaplains from our Armed Forces have been proposed. The end is not yet. Meanwhile, crime, violence, and destructive forces increase.

Population Growth Problem

The rapid increase of world population in the light of food shortages presents an alarming problem.

World population increases fifty million per year—or, to put it another way, increases as a nation the size of Great Britain. Every twenty-four hours world population expands by 150,000.

The population of Southeast Asia doubles every thirty years. The population of Africa doubles every twenty-seven years, and that of South America every twenty-four years.

Smoking

A high-school girl came up and said, "I smoke."

"You're kiddin'."

"Yes, I do smoke."

"I can't believe it."

"But I do."

"Oh, but you don't. The cigarette *smokes;* you're just the *sucker.*"

Satan: The Source of Opposition

The Devil's Best Tool

It was once announced that the devil was going out of business and would offer all tools for sale to whoever would pay his price. On the night of the sale they were all attractively displayed, and a bad-looking lot they were. Malice, Hatred, Envy, Jealousy, Sensuality, and Deceit, and all the other implements of evil were spread out, each marked with its price. Apart from the rest lay a harmless-looking wedge-shaped tool, much worn and priced higher than any of them.

Someone asked the devil what it was.

"That's Discouragement," was the reply.

"Why do you have it priced so high?"

"Because," replied he, "it is more useful to me than any of the others. I can pry open and get inside a man's consciousness with that when I could not get near him with any of the others; and when once inside, I can use him in whatever way suits me best. It is so much worn because I use it with nearly everybody, as very few people yet know it belongs to me."

It hardly need be added that the devil's price of Discouragement was so high that it was never sold. He is still using it.

The Strategy of the Devil

Dean Inge of St. Paul's in London once said:

"History seems to show that the powers of evil have won their greatest triumphs by capturing the organizations which were formed to defeat them and that when the devil has thus changed the contents of the bottles, he never alters the labels. The fort may have been captured by the enemy, but it still flies the flag of its defenders."

At the Devil's Booth

At the devil's booth all things are sold,
Each ounce of dross costs its ounce of gold;
For a cap and bells our lives we pay,
Bubbles we buy with a whole soul's tasking;
'Tis heaven alone that is given away,
'Tis only God may be had for the asking.—*J. R. Lowell*

Social Ills Versus Faith

Year by year social unrest and economic troubles have been mounting in Great Britain. In this connection it is interesting to note that in 1969 only 35 percent of the British people believed in the existence of God, according to a reliable poll. In 1974 the same poll showed that only 29 percent believed that God exists. The attendance at church averages about 3 percent of the population. Is there any relation between declining faith in God and social troubles?

Increase in Alcoholic Consumption

Alcoholic drinking is alarmingly on the increase in our country, if the report of the United States Treasury Department is accepted. This branch of our government reported that for the year 1973 the United States liquor consumption was 4,851,000,000 gallons. This adds up to twenty-three gallons of booze per year for every man, woman, child, and infant in the United States. The money spent for this consumption is $3,100,000 per hour.

Self-righteous or Sinners?

The Catholic Visitor reports that Saint Aloysius Church in Kentucky was having difficulty in getting people to come to a service of confession and penance. As a solution to the low-attendance problem, they put a message on the church bulletin board as follows: "Come, and if you don't have any sins, bring a friend who does."

The Divorce Epidemic

The fever rush to divorce has shot the rate of divorce in the United States to hysterical proportions. According to *New York* magazine, the divorce curve zoomed upwards by 85 percent in the short time between 1963 and 1973. This phenomenal upsurge of 85 percent does not include tens of thousands of couples who have separated but are not yet legally divorced. Divorce is now called "creative" and an "achievement" in personality growth. The majority of divorces occur between the ages of thirty-five and forty-five. To remain married to one man is deplored as "lacking a wide experience in sex." Divorce is now regarded as the "ideal" life-style.

Meanwhile, crumbling family foundations presage instability and moral decay in the nation. No nation survives without secure family life.

18.
Advent—Christmas

Peace at the Heart of Two Great Soldiers

In the history of the tragic War Between the States, no Confederate general except Robert E. Lee and Stonewall Jackson was more popular than George E. Pickett. A flamboyant character, romantic as he was brave, he led the famous charge at the Battle of Gettysburg.

His love and loyalty to his beautiful wife were somehow known to both armies. When his first baby was born, a son, the two armies were drawn up for battle, facing each other. Somehow the news of the popular general's first baby cheered and softened the bitterness of war.

All along the two-mile Confederate battleline, cheers were shouted and bonfires were built in celebration of the event. It was a beautiful sight—the long stretch of bonfires illuminating the thick darkness.

General Grant was curious to know what was happening in the Confederate Army. He sent out scouts to learn the cause. They reported that Mrs. Pickett had just given birth to her first child. The general had a son.

General Grant said, "Haven't we any kindling wood on this side of the line? Why don't we strike up a row of lights, too, for the young Pickett?"

Soon bonfires were blazing all along the Union line. Not a shot was fired; not a gun pointed at an enemy. Bright lights and peace reigned because a baby was born.

A few days later a baby's silver service, engraved to George E. Pickett, Jr., from General Grant and two other other Union generals, was taken through the lines.

Will there come someday such a glorious celebration of the birth of baby Jesus that the wars of earth will be hushed into peace?

God Made Real

It is said of a boy who greatly admired his father, who was in Europe fighting in World War II, that one day he stood for a long time just gazing at his father's picture. As his mother came into the room, he said, "Mother, do you know what I wish could happen? I wish my father could step out of that picture frame and be real to me."

This is what God does for us in Christ: He steps out of the farawayness and the distance and becomes real in a Person.

Essential Ingredient

A frame without a picture,
A name without a face:
Such is the Christmas pageant
Without the Prince of Grace.
A feast with food forgotten,
A jest without the joy,
A night without the dawning:
Christmas without God's Boy.—*Thomas John Carlisle*

Jesus Christ: His Life

Christmas Christians are limited Christians. It might seem safe to try to keep Christ wrapped as a baby and limited to a manger, a cradle, or a crèche. but too much is lost. It is in the context of his life and ministry that Bethlehem has meaning.

Once more the pageant has been seen;
Once more the miracle has come.

We who donned burlap and gauze
Have worn silk:
We who are penniless
Have given gold.

Mere men,
We have been shepherds and angels,
Prophets and kings:
What is more,
We have mingled as friends.

Is there no end
To what the Child can do?

No end!—*Charles A. Waugaman*

19.
Responding to Introductions

After-Dinner Speaker

This has been a sumptuous feast tonight, and I am reminded of what Saint Paul said: "Eat what is set before you, and think not what ye shall put on."

After a Too-Elaborate Introduction

"Mr. Chairman, I'm glad you decided to say nothing about me."

Letting Yourself Down

Recently I was scheduled to speak before a women's club. Just before I was to speak, the alert chairman announced an offering and urged every woman to give generously, for the money was badly needed.

Turning to the lady chairwoman, I ventured to ask politely, "May I ask the purpose of the money you are collecting?"

Unhesitatingly she replied, "Oh, we are raising a fund to secure better speakers for our club."

Somebody

Your chairman is so diplomatic that somehow, in some way, he makes someone feel that he must be somebody even though he may be nobody.

Applause

Thank you for your applause, but I always say to myself: If I am applauded before I begin, that's FAITH. If I am applauded while I am speaking, that's HOPE. If I am applauded when I am all through, that's CHARITY.

A Jaunty Response

I must say, your chairman knows how to sling the applesauce. I think he must be all out of raspberries. You remember the French Canadian picking blueberries in northern Maine, who said, "Dem blueberries makes just as good applesauce as cranberries." Anyway, you know it's all applesauce; but somehow we all like it.

Your Hospitality

I'm thankful that your warm hospitality tonight is not like Scottish but rather like Irish hospitality.

If you attend an English tea and ask for more sugar, your hostess gives you a lump of sugar.

If you attend an Irish tea and ask for more sugar, your hostess passes you the sugar bowl.

But if you attend a tea in Scotland and ask for more sugar, your Scottish hostess looks at you and says, "Are you sure you have *stir-r-red* it?" Your hospitality is in bountiful bowls like the Irish.

Stewardship—Every Bit Helps

There is a story told of a man by the name of Joe Bit. He married a woman; then there were two Bits. They had a baby, and then there were three Bits. In a few years more children came into the family, until there were eight in all.

"How do you manage to support such a large family?" someone asked the father. He replied, "Well, it ain't easy; but every little Bit helps."

Don't Be Taken In

Your chairman was so extravagant in his introduction that I must express the hope that you were not "taken in" by what he said.

I recall by way of his remarks how a nervous young preacher misread the Bible passage about Enoch. The Bible passage actually says, "Enoch was not for God took him." But the nervous preacher, a poor reader at best, fumbled and read instead, "Enoch was not what God took him for."

Length of Speech

A young minister beginning his parish work went to an older minister for advice.

"Can you help me by telling me what to preach about?"

The older minister briefly replied, "Preach about God and about twenty minutes."

No Souls Saved

It is told of President Hadley of Yale that at a chapel service, as he was about to introduce a famous speaker, the speaker leaned over and whispered to the president, "Is there a time limit on how long I may speak?"

"No," said the president, "we set no time limit. But," he added delicately, "I might add that no souls are saved after the first twenty minutes."

When Called on Suddenly

I had not expected to be called on tonight, and I would remind you that the Bible warns, "Lay hands suddenly on no man."

To Be Thought Wise—Silence

Solomon remarked that even a fool, if he holds his tongue, will be esteemed a wise man.

When You Are the Last Speaker

Two Irishmen were discussing the accidents on railroad trains.

Mike said, "Have you noticed how all the accidents always happen on the last car?"

"Well then," said Pat, "why don't they leave off the last car?"

Second Visit—Gratitude

Traveler in Siam met in jungle an elephant which had a deep thorn in foot. Traveler extracted thorn from foot, and elephant disappeared into jungle—later captured and sold to circus in America. Twenty years later this traveler sitting in circus tent in New York, watching parade of elephants. Suddenly something familiar in atmosphere stirred his feelings. At that moment elephant stopped and looked at him. The elephant took long trunk, wrapped end of it affectionately around waist of traveler, and lifted him out of a fifty-cent seat and put him down in a five-dollar seat.

Gratitude is a rare trait, even in elephant. But I have not forgotten your past favors, and I come to express my gratitude tonight.

Introducing a Man of Convictions

Once in Ohio there was a politician who couldn't win the farmers' vote. When a farmer was asked why at a political rally, he stood up and declared: "We won't vote for you because we don't like your convictions."

The politician shot back, "Name them, and I'll change them."

Now our speaker tonight is not like that. He is a man of strong and steadfast convictions.

Important to Get Acquainted

It's a most pleasant experience meeting you today in this formal way, but some things must wait on our getting better acquainted.

I'm reminded of the new neighbor who moved in next door to Mr. and Mrs. John Jones. Mrs. Jones was much interested in the life-style of her new neighbors and even waxed enthusiastic about them to her husband.

"John," she glowed, "you should see what a devoted couple they are. He kisses her every time he goes out, and he even waves kisses to her from the road. Why don't you do that?"

"Why don't I?" retorted John in amazement. "Why, I don't even know her yet."

Use Your Brains

A woman, having just learned to drive, stalled her car in traffic.

An irate cop came alongside and said impatiently, "Lady, use your noodle, use your noodle."

Searching all over the dash panel, she answered anxiously, "Where is it, officer? I can't find it."

When Called to Pinch-Hit

Down South a hillbilly church always had a spring strawberry festival. They had big signs painted and spread all over the town. *"Great Strawberry Festival. Luscious Juicy Strawberries and Cream."*

When people came to the festival, however, having purchased their tickets in advance, they found a sign at the church door. The word "Strawberries" was crossed out, and this sign was in its place. "Due to the recession no strawberries tonight. *Prunes will be served instead."*

I feel sorry for you folks who came tonight expecting strawberries and must put up with prunes instead.

Will Have Attention to Terminal Facilities

In Scotland a stranger in the pews whispered to a deacon beside him,

"Isn't the minister done yet?"

"Yes," said the Scottish deacon, "he's done; but he will not quit."

I intend to quit on time.

Who Will Listen?

1. After listening to this wonderful introduction, I cannot but wish my wife had been here to hear this.

2. After hearing this long and elaborate introduction, I wondered for a moment if I was not listening to my obituary.

3. What a marvelously generous build-up your chairman has given me in his gracious introduction. If I were ever to run for high political office and I could get your chairman for my publicity man, I sure would be bound to win the election.

When a Woman Is Chairman

Madam Chairman, your fascinating charm inspires my memory of a well-known couplet from Shakespeare.

> Breathes there a man with soul so dead
> Who never turned his head and said, ah, not bad.

Response to a Flattering Introduction

Senator Chaucey M. Depew, a well-known wit, was honored at a New York dinner with generous praise.

In responding to the flattery he said, "It is nice to get these generous compliments while I'm still alive. I had rather have the taffy now than the epitaphy later."

Opening Remarks

Introductory Story

Someone had said that the human mind is a wonderful thing. The human brain begins working from the instant you are born and never stops until you get up to make a speech.

Fat Man Adapts to the Situation

Gilbert K. Chesterton, who was an enormously fat man, attended a religious conference held at Letchworth, England, where he was advertised to take the chair of the meeting—which he did in his own original fashion.

Having wedged his big hulk into an armchair of absurdly insufficient size, he then started to speak; but as he stood, the chair rose with him and stuck to him devotedly, despite the efforts of those sitting on either side of him to disengage him from the chair. At last they got the chair loose, and Chesterton began saying, "Now that I am free to speak to you, I am wondering whether I would not have done better to have stuck to the chair. What an ideal chairman I could have made. All I can hope is that I shall adhere to the points at issue in this debate and that we shall get to the bottom of our more pressing problems."

Beginning or End

I hardly know where to begin my speech tonight. As a matter of fact, however, I imagine most of you are hoping that I will know where to end. Anyway, seat yourselves comfortably and prepare for the worst.

When You Are the Last Speaker

In this situation, coming immediately after the eloquent Dr. Blank, I can only quote a well-known Scripture passage, "What can the man do who comes after the King?"

For a Late Hour

My friends, the more I attend conventions the more I'm amazed at the patient endurance of American audiences. I am glad to participate in this marathon endurance contest.

Knowing how late the hour is, I am reminding myself that an address does not need to be interminable in order to be immortal.

20.
Humorous Stories

The Lighter Side

Nothing indicates the greatness of man better than his ability to laugh at himself. Laughter can be as powerful a teaching device as shock.

Courtship and High Aim

A young man was taking home a beautiful young woman after their first date together. At the front door of her home as he was saying his final good-bye, he suddenly felt courageous and put a quick kiss on the girl's chin.

"How do you like that, sweetheart?" he asked.

Her eyes twinkled; she looked down at him and replied, "Very fair, very fair; but why don't you aim higher?"

Don't Be Shy

A rather shy boy driving his auto with his girl on the front seat had long been trying to get up his courage to ask the girl for a kiss. At last he thought of a way.

"Now when I drive past that tenth telephone pole," he exclaimed, "I'm going to kiss you. What do you say to that?"

"Isn't that a little too late?" she answered.

Grounds for Refusal

When a very charming single woman was asked why she had never married, she replied, "I refuse to get married on scriptural grounds." "What Scripture?" her friends asked her. She said, "First Thessalonians 4:13, 'I would not have you—ignorant brethren.' "

When You Come to the Last Item on the Agenda

A maiden lady who had reached her fortieth year had turned down many offers of marriage. Now one more man made her a proposal. Asked why she accepted this time, she answered, "Well, I guess I'm on my last lap."

Marriage Fulfillment

A fellow said, "I never was a self-starter. It doesn't matter much; I'm marrying a crank."

Enough

There is satisfaction in having children. It has been said that a man with ten children is certain to be more satisfied than a man with a million dollars. The man who has a million dollars wants more.

Multiple Returns

Science says a single oyster can lay up to fifty oysters in *one* day—can you imagine what a married oyster can do?

What Do You Want? Service with a Smile

A young ensign was pacing the floor when the glad tidings arrived by telegram. "Maxine gave birth to a little girl this A.M. Both doing nicely." On the message at the bottom was the sticker, "When you want a boy, call Western Union."

Thinking—Old Family Custom

"From 70 to 90 percent of the thinking of the people is ancestral."—*Newton D. Baker*

Childbirth

A young father-to-be was pacing back and forth, wringing his hands in the hospital corridor while his wife was in labor. He was tied up in knots of fear and anxiety, and beads of perspiration dropping from his brow revealed the agony of his suffering. Finally at 4 A.M. a nurse popped out of a door and said, "Well, sir, you have a little girl."

He dropped his hands, became limp, and said, "Oh, how I thank God it's a girl. She'll never have to go through the awful agony I've had tonight."

Word Choice Makes a Difference

It is said that Noah Webster's wife (Noah Webster compiled the famous Webster's Dictionary) once caught him kissing the housemaid.

In condemnation Mrs. Webster exclaimed, "I'm surprised, Noah."

"No, my dear," replied Webster. "I am surprised, but you are astonished."

Praise

Billy Sunday once said, "Try praising your wife, even if it does frighten her at first."

Lies and Liars

A little girl got her Scripture mixed when she quoted, "A lie is an abomination unto the Lord and a very present help in time of trouble." Mark Twain advised, "Always speak the truth—then you'll remember what you said." Dr. Charles Gilkey of Chicago recalls an uncle of his at Islesboro, Maine, sitting by the fireplace and conducting family worship. He read where the psalmist said, "I said in my haste, All men are liars" (Ps. 116:11). The old uncle remarked, "David said this in his haste; but if he had taken time to think about it deeply, he couldn't have come nearer the truth. He wouldn't have had any reason to change his mind."

Little Thomas: A fib is the same as a story, and a story is the same as a lie.

Little Nan: No, it isn't.

Thomas: Yes, it is. My father said so, and my father is an editor.

Nan: I don't care if he is. My father is a real-estate man, and he knows more about lying than your father does.

Behind the Successful Man

Someone has said that behind every successful man is a surprised wife and an amazed mother-in-law.

Explanation

A forest ranger met an Indian riding horseback while his wife walked behind. The ranger said, "How is it I always meet you riding your horse, and your wife walking behind?" The Indian slowly answered, "She no gotem horse."

Mental Limitations

"Oh, doctor," said the wife, "my husband John is wandering in his mind."

"Don't let that worry you," said the doctor, "he can't go very far."

Nothing Missed Yet

A baseball fan took his beautiful young bride to her first big league ball game. He had married her more for her beauty than for her brains. Her grooming took more time than he had expected, and they were late arriving at the ball park. As they were seated she asked, "Dear, I wonder what the score is?"

He looked at the scoreboard and answered, "Nothing to nothing." She settled back comfortably and said, "Good, then we haven't missed anything yet."

Ministers as Money Beggars

A mother of three sons couldn't conceal her concern for their futures. So she consulted a crystal-ball gazer to find out what her sons would become. The gazer said their futures were so horrible she couldn't bear to tell her. The mother insisted. "Tell me the worst."

"Well," said the crystal ball gazer, "your first son will be a murderer, your second son a notorious liar, and your third son an inveterate beggar."

Crushed to the heart, the mother now sought out a minister in order to get consolation. The minister took an optimistic view giving her a different interpretation.

"The first son, the one the gazer called a murderer, will be a doctor or a surgeon.

"The second, the big liar, will be a United States Senator.

"The third, the inveterate money beggar, will be either a Methodist or Baptist minister."

Learning Is Bothersome

Apropos of the weight of expanding knowledge today, there is the story of a young son of a French astronomer. The astronomer had gone to his observatory for the evening, and his young son was struggling with his school homework.

"What do you have to do?" his mother asked sympathetically.

"I have to give a report on the moon; won't you please help me write my report?" he replied.

"How silly to ask me! Ask your father; he's the astronomer," the mother said.

"But I don't want to know that much," the boy retorted.

Josh Billings said, "It is better not to know so much than to know so much that ain't so."

Slip of the Tongue—Father's Day

The teenage son asked his dad for the car for a date.

The father objected exasperatedly, "Son, when I was a teenager my father never allowed me to go out at night and certainly not with the car."

"Gee," said the son, "your father must have been a mean, tough guy, if he was like that."

"I'll have you know," retorted the irate parent, "that I had a lot better father than you have."

Education—How to Learn

A father was driving along in a taxi in New York with his young son; they were visiting the big city. As they drove along the Hudson River, the boy pointed to a ship and said, "Dad, what kind of a ship is that?" The dad said, "I don't know, son." A little later the taxi passed a great monument. "Whose monument is that, Dad?" asked the boy. The father replied, "Search me, son; I really don't know." Looming ahead of them was a great steel bridge. "What's the name of that bridge, Dad?" asked the son. "You got me, son; I don't know." There was a long silence, and finally the boy said, "Dad, I hope you don't mind my asking questions; I hope I'm not bothering you." The father replied with enthusiasm, "Certainly not, son. How else are you going to know anything if you don't ask questions?"

Action Still Possible

A boy brought home a poor report card from school to show his father.

Fortunately for the boy, while rummaging through the attic he found a report card of his father's when he was a boy, and his was a poor report card, too.

So in showing his own report card to his father, before his father had a chance to explode, the boy said, "Well, Dad, you can't say anything. Look at the report card you got when you were a boy."

The father studied his son for a moment or two and then said, "No, son, I can't say anything; but I can do just what my father did when he saw my card."

It Pays to Know Your Bible

In a New England family the father was a strict disciplinarian, even in the matter of family prayers. His young son had been pestering him for a watch. At last the exasperated father said, "Don't ever again mention the word *watch* in my presence."

It was a rule of family prayers that the father would go around the family circle, requiring each one to recite from memory a Bible verse. When he came to the boy his son recited, "And what I say unto you, I say unto all, watch."

Twisting God to Our Desires

A mother listening to her little girl's bedside prayer heard her pray, "Dear God, please make Boston the capitol of Vermont."

Astonished by the strange petition, her mother asked, "Why do you pray for that?"

"Because," answered the child, "that's the way I wrote it down on my examination paper today."

A Matter of Taste

"Don't you wish you was a bird, Jimmy, and could fly way up in the sky?" mused little Jean dreamily.

"Naw!" scorned Jimmy. "I'd ruther be a elephant and squirt water through my nose."

A Child's Reaction to Sunday School

One sympathizes with the little lad who was taken to a dreary Sunday School session by his grandmother. Walking home from the church, the boy said, "Grandma, did you ever go to the circus?" She replied, "No, I never went to the circus. But why do you ask?" "Because," he said, "if you ever went to the circus, you would never want to go to that Sunday School again in your life."

Offering Story

A little girl was showing a visitor over her father's farm. She proudly pointed to a cow which was her very own.

"And does your cow give milk?" asked the visitor.

"Well, not exactly," replied the child. "You've sort of got to take it away from her."

Keep a Clear Head

A child was asked the old cathechism question, " 'What is the chief end of man?' " and replied, "The end with the head on."

Embarrassed

The busy mother left her little daughter Mary to fix a light lunch. When the mother returned from her errands with a friend, she noticed that Mary had already strained the tea.

"Oh, did you find the lost strainer?" her mother asked.

"No, Mother, I couldn't find it; so I used the flyswatter."

Her mother nearly swooned. Mary could see she was terribly troubled, so she added, "Don't get excited, Mother. I used the old swatter."

Baptists Take Precedence

A prominent Baptist minister saw his eight-year-old son fighting with another boy. The father went over and pulled him off the other boy and said, "Look here, son, this isn't right. Don't you know you're supposed to be a Christian?" The boy retorted, "I am not a Christian. I'm a Baptist."

Our Wives

A mother told an audience that her little son, on his first day at Sunday School, had been vividly impressed by the story of the creation of woman. He learned that when God wanted Adam to have a wife, he took out one of Adam's ribs and made it into his wife Eve.

That Sunday afternoon he ran a race with boys in the neighborhood and came into the house all out of breath and exhausted. Putting his hand on his rib cage, he said, "Mommy, I've got a big pain. I think I'm going to have a wife."

The Lighter Side of Prayer

A touch of humor is often the best mirror in which to catch a glimpse of our serious mistakes. The realm of prayer is no exception.

Adapting Grace Before Meals

An English clergyman, very fastidious about his food and really a gourmet, changed his grace before meals according to the house where he chanced to be and the food which happened to be served. Before offering the blessing this parson would give a quick glance over the table and another at the sideboard. If the prospects were good for a hearty and delicious meal, he would begin his blessing saying, "Bountiful Father." But if the prospects were not good and he sensed only a meager meal, he would adopt a milder form of grace and say, "For these and for the least of all thy mercies we would thank thee."

Table Grace Can Be Dangerous

The mother was entertaining guests from the church. At dinner she asked the minister guest to say the grace. He was a great lover of children and said, "I think I would enjoy a child's blessing. Would your little son Jimmy say the grace for us?" Five-year-old Jimmy looked up at his mother in helplessness. "I don't know what to say, Mommy."

"Well, you try," said his mother. "Just say what you have heard Mommy say."

He bowed his head and prayed, "Good Lord, why did I ever invite these people here today?"

No Grace at Table

A very young but outspoken lad from a Christian family was invited out to dinner at a neighbor's with his parents.

When no grace was offered the astonished boy said, "You start right in to eat, don't you, just like my dog."

Anticipation

A traveling circus offered a $100 prize to any man who would enter the lion's cage and stay with the lion for five minutes.

A poor preacher, in need of money, remembered Daniel in the lion's den and decided to accept the offer.

But once inside the cage and face to face with the lion, he backed into a corner; and the lion followed him. The preacher, trembling, fell to his knees and, folding his hands, prayed, "Oh, Lord, don't let this lion devour me. Save me from this ferocious beast."

When the preacher opened his eyes he was astonished to see the lion kneeling and his front paws folded in an attitude of prayer.

"What are you praying for?" the preacher asked.

"I'm giving thanks for what I am about to receive," said the drooling lion.

Prayer Meetings No More

One pastor sharing parish problems with another said, "Well, we've given up prayer meetings at our church."

"Why?" asked his friend.

"Only a few faithful aged sisters were attending."

"But what did your deacons say?" inquired the friend.

"Oh, the deacons. Well, they haven't found it out yet."

Prayer Is to God

A reporter on the staff of a Boston newspaper was asked to report on the pulpit appearance of a famous visiting preacher.

In his Monday column he reported that "the famous Dr. Blank offered the most eloquent prayer ever offered to a Boston audience."

Sincerity in Prayer

When Dick Shepard, rector of St. Martins-in-the-Field, London, was attending a prayer meeting, he heard a young minister pompously pray, "O Lord, reveal thyself to us all the panoply of thy eschatological glory." Secretly, within himself, Shepard prayed, "God, who made me simple, make me simpler yet."

Pray for Our Country

The chaplain of the House of Representatives was once asked, "Do you pray for the congressmen?"

He slyly replied, "No, I look at the congressmen and then I pray for the country."

A Child's Prayer

One night I listened to my little daughter Marcia's prayer. She had had a hard day. Her older sister had bossed her; her brother had stolen her hair ribbon; her mother had spanked her; and the teacher had scolded her. As I listened to her bedtime prayer for her dog "Pat," her friends, the poor, and the sick, she ended her prayer with this petition: "Help all the bad people to be good and help all the good people (and then a sob) if there are any." Even in a minister's family, she began to doubt if any good people were left.

Sometimes in a cynical mood we all feel this way about the church members.

Ask Right and It Shall Be Given

It so happened that the radio announced the first B-29 air raid on Japan the afternoon before my little son Arthur's birthday. When Arthur knelt by his bed that night to say his prayers, he said in a very loud voice, "And please, God, send me a very big model B-29 for my birthday present!"

"But you don't have to shout like that," I protested. "God isn't deaf, you know."

"No," replied Arthur. "But Grandpa is, and he's the only guy around here with money enough to get me one."

Adequate for the Occasion

Dr. Maurice Trimmer of West Virginia tells of a young boy listening to men in a country general store. The men were swapping stories. The boy became more and more interested as he leaned his elbow on the molasses barrel. Finally, he became so intense that his elbow slipped into the molasses. He held up his arm, his elbow dripping with yellow molasses, luscious to a boy's eye. He was heard to pray, "Oh Lord, give me a tongue big enough for this occasion!"

Minister's Son's Prayer

A little boy much devoted to his father, who was a pastor, prayed this prayer: "Dear God, help Daddy preach and help him to perspire people."

Dying Editor and Circulation

An editor was dying, and the doctor was called. Feeling his pulse, the doctor said, "His circulation is almost gone." On hearing that, the editor rose up on one elbow and said, "Drive that man out of my house; my circulation is over four hundred thousand."

Importance of the Right Leadership

The other day my little granddaughter asked me, "What part of an automobile causes the most accidents?" I told her I didn't know. She replied, "It's the nut at the wheel."

These Foolish Days

"This song about bananas makes me sick," said the foolish old gentleman. "In my day we had songs like 'Ta Ra Ra Boom De Ay' and 'Daddy Wouldn't Buy Me a Bow-wow,' that had some sense to 'em."

Old Age

Two very old men on a Sunday afternoon were walking in the town cemetery among the headstones and monuments.

"How old are you, Ephraim?"

Eph replied, "Well I'm eighty-eight—going on eighty-nine. How old are you, Zeph?"

Zeph answered, "Well, I'm just ninety-six."

Eph commented, "Well, at your age it hardly pays for you to go home."

Family Life

A precocious child had been disciplined by her mother's teaching to keep family quarrels strictly private. One day this child had been unusually naughty.

"You must be sure to ask God to forgive you for your naughtiness. Did you tell him about your being bad?" the mother asked.

"No," the little girl replied, "I didn't because I knew you wouldn't want anyone outside the family to know about such a scandal."

Mistaken Identity

In an ascending elevator in one of the large department stores in Oakland, California, there were, among others, a woman with her small daughter. Immediately in front of the little girl there was a rather large woman, and alongside of this woman was a man, who apparently was not her husband. Just before arriving at a floor stop the large woman turned suddenly toward the man and violently slapped him in the face, much to his consternation and surprise. The large woman left the elevator at the next stop. The little girl then turned to her mother and said, "I am glad that woman got out. I didn't like her, so I bit her."

Only Fiction—Fallacy

In Boston a youth went into the bookstore and asked the clerk, "Have you a book called *Man, the Master of Women?*" The pretty salesgirl merely tossed her head and said, "You'll have to look for that in the Fiction

Department."

Criticism of Youth Rebuked

A somewhat prudish woman at the beach met a teenager attired only in a brief bikini. Shocked to see so much skin, she stopped the girl and reprimanded her.

"Young lady, I think you ought to be ashamed of yourself going around in that bikini. What would your mother say if she saw you now?"

"She'd be mad as a hornet," the girl replied. "I'm wearing her bikini."

Adulthood

There are many serious definitions of what an adult is. But a humorous definition says that an "adult" is one who stops growing at both ends, while he expands in the middle.

Time Off

A man often celebrates his birthday by taking a day off. Most women, however, prefer to take a year off.

Learn a Second Language

A mama mouse was leading ten of her family of little mice across the kitchen floor.

Suddenly there was a big black cat bearing down on them.

Mama Mouse opened her mouth wide and barked like a dog. The cat skidattled.

Turning to her baby mice, Mama Mouse said, "There, you see how important it is to know a second language."

Ignorance Not Bliss

Mother: "Well, son, what have you been doing all afternoon?"

Son: "Shooting craps."

Mother: "That must stop. Those little things have as much right to live as you have."

This Is No Picnic

The mother of twelve children was being helped onto the bus by the stranger behind her. "Madam, are these all yours, or is this a Sunday School picnic?"

She answered, "They are all mine, and it's no picnic."

As the man who had thirteen children said, "It's the little things in life that count."

Takes Time

Meeting for the first time in years and exchanging reminiscences, two old friends asked a lot of questions.

"Tell me," one friend said to the other, "is your wife Betty just as beautiful as she used to be?"

"Oh yes," his friend replied, "just as beautiful, only now it takes her much longer."

Short Dresses

Most husbands wouldn't object to their wives wearing their dresses a little shorter, if only they would wear them a little longer.

A Toast to Women's Lib

A TV street reporter interviewed a number of the Jesus people in California.

He asked two of these young Christians how many wives a man should have.

One young Christian was confused, for he said that David had several wives and Solomon had many more.

But the other young Christian said positively that a man should have only one wife, and he could prove it from the Bible.

"How is that?" asked the interviewer.

"Because the Bible says, 'No man can serve two masters.' "

College Bred—Ingredients

Small boy: What is college bred, Pop?

Pop (with son in college): They make college bred, my boy, with the flower of youth and the dough of old age.

Wedding Anniversary

Celebrating their fortieth wedding anniversary, Dad and Mom received the following telegram from their son in Hollywood, California. "Congratulations. Dad, is marriage a failure?" The father wired back, "No, but the results of it sometimes are."